WHERE'S MY JETPACK?

WHERE'S MY JETPACK?

A GUIDE TO THE AMAZING SCIENCE FICTION FUTURE THAT NEVER ARRIVED

Daniel H. Wilson, Ph.D.

Illustrated by Richard Horne

BLOOMSBURY

Published by Bloomsbury USA, New York
Distributed to the trade by Holtzbrinck Publishers

All papers used by Bloomsbury USA are natural, recyclable products
made from wood grown in well-managed forests. The manufacturing
processes conform to the environmental regulations of the country of origin.

Library of Congress Cataloging-in-Publication Data

Wilson, Daniel H. (Daniel Howard), 1978– Where's my jetpack?:
a guide to the amazing science fiction future that never arrived / Daniel H. Wilson.
1st U.S. ed. p. cm.

ISBN-10 1-59691-136-0   ISBN-13 978-1-59691-136-9

1. Inventions—Miscellanea. 2. Inventions—History. 3. Inventions—Humor. 4. Forecasting—Miscellanea.
I. Title. II. Title: Where's my jetpack?, a guide to the amazing science fiction future that never arrived.
III. Title: Amazing science fiction future that never arrived.

T49.5.W546 2007   600—dc22   2006021683

Designed and typeset by Richard Horne
Printed in China by South China Printing Co.

www.whereismyjetpack.com

FOR

PAMELA KAYE & DENNIS JAY

WHERE'S MY JETPACK?

SUPERHUMAN ABILITIES

THE HOME OF THE FUTURE

HUMANS ... IN SPACE!

CONCLUSION

ACKNOWLEDGMENTS

INTRODUCTION

The future is now, and we are not impressed. The future was supposed to be a fully automated, atomic-powered, germ-free Utopia — a place where a grown man could wear a velvet spandex unitard and not be laughed at. Our beloved scientists may be building the future, but some key pieces are missing. Where are the ray guns, the flying cars, and the hoverboards that we expected? We can't wait another minute for the future to arrive. The time has come to hold the golden age of science fiction accountable for its fantastic promises.

At the turn of the nineteenth century, visionaries like Jules Verne and H. G. Wells spun wild tales of spaceflight and underwater adventure. In 1926, Hugo Gernsback introduced the first magazine devoted entirely to science fiction, *Amazing Stories*, with the motto "Extravagant Fiction Today: Cold Fact Tomorrow." By midcentury, the Apollo moon missions were gasoline on the flames. As science conquered nature, an optimistic populace yearned to live in the perfect tomorrow. Yet today zeppelins the size of ocean liners do not hover over fully enclosed skyscraper cities. Shiny robot servants do not cook breakfast for colonists on the moon. Worst of all, sleek titanium jetpacks are not ready and waiting on showroom floors.

Every vivid drawing on the cover of a pulp sci-fi magazine was a promise of a better tomorrow, and the

purpose of this book is to deliver on those promises. This book ruthlessly exposes technology, spotlighting existing prototypes and revealing drawing-board plans. You will learn which technologies are already available, who made them, and where to find them. If the technology is not public, you will learn how to build, buy, or steal it. When the technology of yesterday's tomorrow does not yet exist, you will learn what barriers stand in the way of making it real. Be careful, you are holding a hand-sized powder keg of information.

Let's face it, there are myriad ways in which futuristic technology could cause personal injury, societal instability, or explosive decompression. A person would have to be crazier than a trainload of monkeys to want to unleash all this technology at once. Nevertheless, this book solemnly pledges to completely ignore any potentially catastrophic consequences of worldwide technology adoption. If the technology is possible — even remotely so — this book will lay it out for all to see.

Despite every World's Fair prediction, every futuristic ride at Disneyland, and the advertisements on the last page of every comic book ever written, we are not living in a techno-Utopia. Not yet. Now is the time to stop wishing, to stand up, and to shout, **"Where the hell is my jetpack!?"**

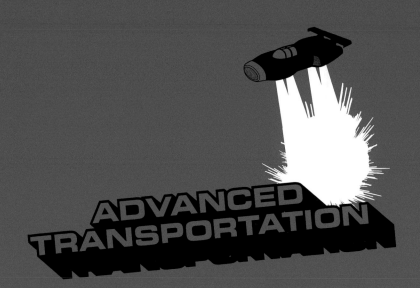

ADVANCED
TRANSPORTATION

JETPACK

It is the last thing you think about before going to sleep. It is the first thing you think of when you wake up. It is a streamlined, curiously heavy bundle of technology with two shoulder straps and one gift to humankind — the gift of flight. The personal jetpack is the holy grail of classic science fiction technology, the ultimate birthday present on steroids, and best of all, the personal jetpack exists.

It all began in 1928, when Buck Rogers ostensibly appeared in an issue of *Amazing Stories* powering through the sky with help from a hot new jetpack. In 1939 a movie came out with Buck flying by virtue of a "degravity belt." The "atomic rocket pack" made a comeback in the 1949 movie *King of the Rocket Men*. No matter what you call it, old Buck was sporting the coolest toy the world has ever seen; his appearances aroused techno-lust in thousands of people and inspired generations of intrepid inventors to attempt to build their very own jetpacks.

The jetpack is just that — a backpack with jet thrusters ready to launch a human skyward at the jiggle of a finger. It is a deceptively simple idea, but it took a team of rocket scientists to create the first working jetpack (technically a rocket pack). Wendell Moore of Bell Aerosystems Company finished the "Bell Rocket Belt" in 1961. The momentous invention was straightforward: Moore mounted a rocket onto a backpack and tested the device all by himself (with a strong tether to prevent any unwanted trips into the atmosphere). The rocket, called a *small rocket lift device*, was similar to one used on the tail and wingtips of an experimental plane to help the pilot maintain control at high altitudes (where thin air hampers normal aerodynamic flight characteristics). Moore's foray into science fiction produced a fully functional rocket-powered backpack — and it never even underwent any monkey test trials.

Conceptually, the Bell rocketbelt is simple; it hovers in the air by forcing gas at high pressure through two downward-facing steel exhaust tubes. Power is generated by a throttleable rocket motor that runs on six gallons of hydrogen peroxide, a clear dense liquid commonly used in bleaches, disinfectants, and antiseptics. The bleach under your sink uses a hydrogen peroxide concentration of about 3 percent, but the rocketbelt uses around 90 percent, which makes it highly volatile. The rocketbelt has three fuel tanks; two outer tanks contain hydrogen peroxide propellant and a middle tank contains nitrogen. When the pilot opens the throttle, nitrogen is released into the outer fuel tanks, forcing the hydrogen peroxide at high pressure over a catalyst bed of fine-mesh silver screens. The mixture of hydrogen peroxide and silver causes an expanding reaction, producing a jet of superheated steam that fires out of the rocket nozzles at high velocity, launching the rocketbelt into the sky. The contraption is only three feet long, but it produces around 300 pounds of thrust (just enough to lift a person and a jetpack).

While the roaring rocketbelt could propel a screaming human to 60 mph in seconds, the fuel lasted for only about half a minute — which led to more screaming. With no parachute and a short flight time, pilots faced a gruesome death with every rocketbelt flight. Eventually, designers affixed a vibrating box to the helmet; after ten seconds it vibrated intermittently and after fifteen seconds it vibrated continuously to let the pilot know it was time to land or die. Despite a few serious injuries (including Wendell Moore's shattered knee), no rocketbelt pilots were ever killed en route. For several decades, the rocketbelt and her sister copies were flown for fun and profit, including in the 1965 James Bond movie, *Thunderball*, and at the 1984 summer Olympic Games in Los Angeles.

However, since the 1960s there has been a startling lack of innovation in personal jetpack technology. Almost every inventor, amateur or otherwise, has sought to copy the Bell Rocket Belt, even though it's impacted by a severely limited flight time and prohibitively expensive fuel. Three outfits have working rocketbelt copycats: the GoFast rocketbelt promotes a sports drink; Juan Lozano is a Mexican with a dream (and two self-built rocketbelts for sale); and Powerhouse Productions provides two rocketbelts for performances (with celebrity stunt doubles on request). But harnessing a controlled explosion in a backpack is no simple task, and almost every amateur attempt has failed. In the 1990s two business partners built and demonstrated a working copy of the original rocketbelt, called the Rocketbelt 2000 (a.k.a. the RB 2000 "Pretty Bird"). Alas, discord broke out between the partners, and after a hammer attack, a kidnapping, and a murder, one partner disassembled the prototype and hid the pieces. The RB 2000 has never been found. If Wendell Moore could see the state of jetpacks today, he would be doing barrel rolls in his grave.

Despite a high-flying past, the options for obtaining a newly built rocketbelt today are next to nil. However, anyone interested in *borrowing* a rocketbelt and making a daring twenty-five-second escape is in luck — six Bell Rocket Belts were built and four remain. The A1 Army Rocketbelt is exhibited at the U.S. Army Transportation Museum at Fort Eustis, Virginia. Two more are on display at the Niagara Aerospace Museum (one real and one a mock-up). Another rocketbelt is featured at the Engineering Department of the State University of New York, at Buffalo, and one is at the Smithsonian's National Air and Space Museum. The other rocketbelt was disassembled and used to build another failed flying device. Of course, "liberating" a jetpack is not much use if you can't fly it.

A sonic boom is continuously produced while an object travels above the speed of sound, not just when the object breaks the sound barrier.

Welcome to Rocketbelts 101. The rocketbelt is framed by dull-gray metal, has shiny foil insulation around the rocket nozzles, and holds three smooth white gas tanks. From a distance it looks like an external-frame rucksack with white scuba tanks attached. Once you have it in your hands, pull the rig onto your back like a backpack and tighten the shoulder straps. (Lift with your legs — the fully fueled rocketbelt weighs about 125 pounds.) Now grab the two metal bars jutting from under your arms by the motorcycle-style handgrips. If your ears are unprotected, prepare to lose some hearing — the rocket engine is deafeningly loud. Also, the exhaust is over 1,300 degrees Farenheit. You did remember to wear a flashy, heat-resistant body suit, right? Twist the right handgrip to start the engine and throttle up. Steer by leaning your body and by twisting the left grip, which pivots the rocket nozzles forward and backward. Now, make your escape! (Be sure to bend your knees upon landing and don't be embarrassed if you fall on your back — it happens to even the best pilots.)

Stealing an antiquated rocketbelt is not advised; why not steal an antiquated *jetbelt* instead? Just before his death in 1969, the father of the rocketbelt constructed and tested a jet-powered jetbelt. With a scant three-million-dollar investment from the Defense Advanced Research Projects Agency (DARPA), Moore promised a jetpack capable of speeds up to 85 mph and a flight time of twenty-five minutes. The final device looked like an inverted jet engine attached to a backpack. This jetpack came with a parachute — to save pilot and jetbelt in case of catastrophic failure at great height. In its first untethered run the jetbelt negotiated a 300-foot-long course while 25 feet in the air, reaching 30 mph. Soon after, the jetbelt appeared in an Ovaltine advertisement. Unfortunately, Moore suffered a heart attack and died unexpectedly. Bell, having failed to attract military or commercial interest, shut down the project and sold the plans to Williams Research Corporation. The jetbelt was lost to time.

The development of the jetpack effectively ceased the day Wendell Moore passed away, and there are plenty of reasons why. As it turns out, the government frowns on the notion of everyday people equipped with jetpacks and the ensuing midair collisions, air rage, and transformation of drunk drivers into inebriated human torpedoes. Worse yet, jetpacks are nearly useless in military applications — a soldier strapped to a jetpack is a sitting duck. The sad truth is that there is no good reason for government or major industry to fund the development of a jetpack. Apparently, inspiring childlike awe does not count as a good reason.

You don't need a triple Ph.D. to know that a working jetpack would be the ultimate technological achievement of humankind. Somehow, it seems that the sheer exhilirating joy of soaring skyward while strapped to a thundering mechanical backpack could never become mundane, even if you clutched a fast-food burger in one hand and the throttle in the other. Alas, personal jetpacks will probably never be a part of our daily lives, but they will surely pay off for advertisers and extreme sports afficionados. Who knows, maybe a new class of extreme jetpackers will populate future soft-drink commercials. Wherever a dangerous new technology exists, there is a guy with cool goggles and streaky blonde hair waiting to shatter his fibula. Totally.

MOON SPACE AVAILABLE

WHERE'S MY JETPACK?

ZEPPELIN

Aviators of the past imagined behemoth airships that could float silently between skyscrapers — and then they built them. In the 1930s, giant dirigibles (three times the size of a Boeing 747 jumbo jet) routinely ran intercontinental routes. Humankind's very first aircraft began as a simple bag of gas and evolved into a Zeppelin-class military superweapon before fading into obscurity. Today, we are on the cusp of rediscovering the most impressive — and massive — technology the skies of Earth have ever known.

Lighter-than-air ships have come a long way since 1783, when the Montgolfier brothers ascended in a fragile, unsteerable *free ballon* — 120 years before the Wright brothers took flight, incidentally. In the following centuries, simple ballons evolved into steerable airships with rigid structural skeletons. The famous German aeronaut Count von Zeppelin designed the first *rigid frame* airship, known as the *Zeppelin*, just in time for World War I (circa 1914). Over the next half century, 119 zeppelins were built, including the *Graf Zeppelin* and the infamous *Hindenburg*.

Beneath its skin, a zeppelin was divided into self-contained air cells, most of which were filled with hydrogen gas and wired into place. (Hydrogen is extremely flammable, but the safer helium gas was not available to the Germans during WWI or WWII.) Gas bags were made of lightweight silk and lined with airtight *gold-beater's skin,* a membrane harvested from cow guts. Count von Zeppelin passed away before WWI began, but his zeppelin airships entered battle against England as strategic air bombers. When the British countered with incendiary bullets — designed to ignite the hydrogen-filled monsters overhead — Germany responded with *height-climbers,* stripped-down airships capable of soaring up to 20,000 feet in the sky (a nosebleed altitude well above the bullet and fighter plane range of the day). During World War I the damage caused by airships was mostly psychological; they were just too slow and inefficient to be used effectively in battle. By World War II balloons were commonly used for patrolling, hunting submarines, and escorting ships, but the age of the war blimp was over. Instead, the next round of luxury airships became propaganda tools for Hitler and the Nazi Party.

Blimpin' ain't easy, but the ostentatious airship of yesteryear was one sweet ride. Here's why you would claw out a flight attendant's eyes for a trip on the ill-fated *Hindenburg:* At a mind-blowing 804 feet long, the airship was the biggest and most luxurious human-made object ever to fly. It was about eight times longer than a puny blue whale (take that, nature). The public lounge, dining rooms, and observation areas provided space to roam;

there was no need for instructive flyers on how to perform phony in-seat yoga exercises. From your stateroom window (many of which could be opened) you could watch the ground skimming below at between 400 and 800 feet — low enough to see the reactions of the people you might spit on. After taking a shower and feeding your nicotine addiction in the smoking room, you could partake in a gourmet dinner in a full dining room with *real* plates and cutlery. And it was not as dangerous as you might think; the airship completed ten round-trips over the North Atlantic and eight over the South Atlantic without complications. When the *Hindenburg* tragically exploded in flames on May 6, 1937 (official cause: buildup of static electricity igniting leaking hydrogen gas), rescuers were thankfully able to save 62 of the 97 passengers.

Though fiery explosions brought on the demise of commercial airships, a simple fact remains: Someday, the fate of the free world may rest solely upon your ability to pilot a stolen Nazi zeppelin. Remember, you are commanding an airship that stretches longer than a city block, flaunts an embarrassing 45-foot-wide swastika emblem that is visible for miles, and is filled with several million cubic feet of flammable hydrogen gas. The slightest change in barometric pressure, humidity, or air temperature will alter the gross lift of your airship. A rule of thumb: Lift is greater in cold weather and lower in sunny climes. If the airship is too heavy, drop your water ballast and shower the countryside with rain (easily more than 5 tons). If the ship is too light, valve your hydrogen reserves into the atmosphere and lose some altitude. Alternately, throttle those engines and nose the great airship toward the ground to maintain altitude when you are too light or toward the sky when you are too heavy. Your top speed is 77 mph on a clear day. Maintain a low altitude and keep a sharp eye out for stormy weather — gale-force winds could rip off your rudder, which is the size of an ice-skating rink (it happened to the *Macon* airship in 1935). Also, please be advised that federal regulations prohibit lighting up outside of the smoking room of the airship. Commander, we salute you and your faithful crew!

Altitude measurements were often made from the *Hindenburg* by dropping glass bottles and judging the amount of time before they shattered on the ground below.

Now let's face harsh reality — you may think you can fly one, but there are no more existing massive rigid-frame airships. All airships flying today are smaller *nonrigid* blimps, meaning that their shape is maintained by internal gas pressure alone. Modern blimps make up for their diminutive size with advanced technology — the helium-filled Goodyear blimp is computer-controlled by two pilots, unlike the *Hindenburg*, which required a crew of thirty-five men who communicated by telephone! Taking a cue from Adolf Hitler, Goodyear uses its fleet of airships solely for propaganda purposes; they generally carry only a handful of passengers and not only are the blimps themselves mega-billboards, but they are also festooned with other advertisements and feature full-color, live video. Advertising is the sole job of today's blimps, but what about tomorrow's?

As usual, the U.S. military is making sure that the wild promises of pulp science fiction magazines are kept. The Pentagon's Missile Defense Agency is funding development of what appears to be one bad robot blimp, ostensibly to keep America's pristine shores free of filthy terrorist missiles. Specifications are classified, but plans call for a "high-altitude unmanned airship" that is seventeen times larger than the Goodyear blimp. The airship is designed to ascend to 60,000 feet (over 10 miles) and hover there for months at a time. Not to be outdone, DARPA has launched the Walrus program, which calls for a superlarge heavy-lift air vehicle designed to deliver an 1,800-person "Unit of Action" to unimproved landing sites. In between "persistence missions" (i.e., monitoring battles), the stalwart airship will be able to haul 500 tons (that's around 400 full-grown walruses) more than halfway around the planet in less than a week. When you tire of watching football from the Goodyear blimp, just switch the channel and watch World War III from the Walrus-cam.

But not all blimps are so bellicose; lucky for you, a new generation of luxury airships are also back on the radar. The decadent *Aeroscraft* (prototype due in 2010) is a modern transoceanic passenger airship in the tradition of the *Graf Zeppelin*. Filled with insert helium and longer than two football fields, the airship will tote an acre-sized cabin that is slated to contain extravagant staterooms, restaurants, and even a casino. It will be a great place for Indiana Jones to stage a fistfight. Helium lifts only about 90 percent as well as hydrogen does, so unlike a zeppelin, the Aeroscraft will contain only enough gas to support two thirds of its overall weight — the rest of the lift will be generated by six turbofan jet engines and an aerodynamic hull. This albino whale with windows is expected to cruise at 174 mph and be able to cross North America three times on one tank of gas, so to speak.

Although the drawing boards are full of burgeoning blimps, the news for now is grim — despite the development of commercial blimps and military airships, your chance of boarding a rigid airship anytime soon is slim. Your chances of entering the Air Force and emerging as a zeppelin fighter ace are even slimmer. We must each decide on our own whether life is worth living without the prospect of a relaxed cruise in a luxurious airship the size of a small Mexican village. Sadly, these amazing leviathans of the sky are still "currently under construction" — just like your home page.

MOVING SIDEWALK

The future of the past was a strange land where automobiles were banished to the skies and mighty pedestrians roamed the Earth, holding dominion over all that was underfoot. The 1964 World's Fair exhibit City of the Future was a supersized technological paradise sprinkled with mile-high skyscrapers and swarms of ant-sized people. The city was huge, but not too huge for itty-bitty, enterprising human beings. Its vast distances were tamed by the hallmark of pedestrian land dominance — the moving sidewalk (also known as a people mover, a rolling road, a travelator, or an electric slidewalk).

The first notion of "rolling roads" sprang from H. G. Wells in his 1899 novel, *When the Sleeper Wakes*. Wells proposed a perpetually moving wooden roadway, complete with seats and tables. Although the futuristic vision of a road could hypothetically negotiate curves, the idea is still reminiscent of two tickets' worth of a spook ride at the county fair. By 1940 the concept was taken further by Robert Heinlein in his story "The Roads Must Roll." Heinlein stepped it up by envisioning a sliding pavement that moved at a brisk 100 mph. Obviously, stepping onto a strip of speeding pavement from a dead stop would put a dent in your grill, so Heinlein described a series of strips that traveled at faster and faster speeds. Falling from one strip to another would be about as damaging as taking a spill off an exercise machine.

Reaching the center lane of this mechanized superhighway, however, would make life worth living.

Today, people movers are real and even mundane. The technology is known as a "passenger conveyor belt" and the first one was installed in 1954 by Goodyear for the Hudson and Manhattan Railroad. Since then, people movers have become a familiar sight at most airports. The most common passenger conveyor belt is built by Westmont Industries and is called the *Speedwalk* (used for flat surfaces) or the *Speedramp* (used for inclines). The device is highly customizable; it can be up to four and a half feet wide and one and a half times longer than a football field. During the ride, one is free to grasp the moving handrail for support, or to smash the emergency stop button if one's pants are being pulled down into the gaping maw of the machine. (Actually, new models are equipped with a "comb-plate sensor" to prevent maulings.) Ultimately, this commonly used treadway will drag a standing passenger along at a disappointing 1.5 mph (about half the average walking speed).

The sluggish top speed of

conventional people movers is limited because the entire treadmill runs at a single constant rate. This means that the top speed of the conveyor belt is determined by the safest entry speed, which is not very fast. If a constant-rate treadmill were to move faster than about 1.5 mph, then an unacceptable number of people would perform painful somersaults when stepping onto the moving metal treads. The solution, as always, is to listen to a science fiction author — much like in Heinlein's vision, high-tech passenger conveyor belts employ multiple strips that move at different speeds. Variable-speed people pushers will get you there fast; just bring along a pair of wind goggles.

Designed over the last few years, these higher-speed slidewalks use a series of belts that are placed end to end and that roll at gradually increasing speeds. Different parts of a single walkway move at different speeds, with the fastest track in the middle of the ride. At the end of this jaunt look forward to a similar deceleration process — along with highly annoying safety messages played on an endless loop.

Variable-speed moving walkways are

rare, but they can seriously cruise. The promisingly named TurboTrack walkway rolls at about 4.5 mph and was recently unveiled by ThyssenKrupp, a German industrial conglomerate. Introduced in 2002, the *trottoir roulant rapide* ("fast-moving sidewalk") in Paris is over 600 feet long and originally used a 30-foot-long accelerator track to propel people up to 7.5 mph. Due to a series of what must have been hilarious injuries, the system currently ships 110,000 people a day through the Montparnasse Metro station at a more sober 3 mph. Operating at its fastest setting, the speedy sidewalk could enable an average person to haul ass at over 20 mph — about as fast as an Olympic sprinter.

> **In 1898, terrified shoppers who came to see the newly installed escalators at Harrods received smelling salts and brandy.**

Over a century after the idea was first introduced, we are just scratching the surface of what is possible. Proponents note that moving sidewalks are cheaper and easier to maintain than subways or tramways. For now, however, a few litigious pedestrians have spoiled it for the rest of us with their skull-cracking falls and attendant lawsuits. But once additional safety measures are established, the future may be a place where speeding pedestrians can race automobiles for fun. Now we just need to get to work on building those monolithic, windowless buildings.

WHERE'S MY JETPACK?

YOU
ARE
HERE

SELF-STEERING CAR

In the idealistic, post-WWI-induced visions of the future, every city was riddled with floating highways populated by ultrafast, self-steering automobiles. The evolution of the automobile was aimed toward slotted tracks that would process cars automatically. Today, highways still do not float, but cars *are* driving themselves. Whether on winding European roadways or across the California deserts, robotic cars are cruising solo.

Good news: At last, the formerly fantastic visions of the automatic car have come true. Siemens Corporation has already installed self-steering buses in many western European cities, including Cambridge, England, and Rouen, France. The self-steering buses help drivers negotiate ancient roads that are too narrow and dangerous for ordinary buses driven by ordinary humans with ordinary reflexes. These robotic buses come equipped with reflexes of their own.

Siemens's self-steering buses have eyes; they use a camera mounted at the top of the windshield to follow ordinary lines painted on the road. The system works like this: A camera sees roughly a hundred yards ahead and alerts the driver that the automatic system is in control by vibrating the steering wheel. The human driver can then let go of the wheel entirely, although he or she continues to control acceleration and braking, and can override the system at any time to avoid obstacles. As long as the road lines are visible, the superior robot-guided buses are guaranteed to maintain a millimeter-precision course, allowing cyclists and pedestrians to pass as close as they like without fear that the driver will veer suddenly. When the road lines are obscured by snow or fog, however, watch out! The almost (but not quite) obsolete human driver must once again take control.

Self-steering vehicles are not reserved exclusively for European bus drivers. Late-model American automobiles incorporate a plethora of automatic driving features. The 2005 Acura RL is voice-activated and can give directions or find locations via a normal conversation. (And you thought that only *Knight Rider*'s David Hasselhoff could talk to his car!) Meanwhile, the 2007 Lexus LS 460 boasts "Intelligent Park Assist" — just target a spot and the car uses radar to park itself; all you have to do is keep your foot lightly on the brake. The new Honda Accord comes with the Advanced Driver Assist System (ADAS), which is essentially a "car copilot" that uses a camera and radar to automatically steer and accelerate on the highway. ADAS has two subsystems: Adaptive Cruise Control uses a radar pulse to scan ahead for other vehicles and it increases or decreases the car's speed accordingly. The Lane Keep Assist System uses a camera placed next to the rearview mirror to monitor the white lines along highways and uses the data to subtly steer the car toward the center of the lane. Don't give in to the temptation to climb into the back seat for a snooze — drivers with ADAS must remain in their seats and touch the steering wheel every ten seconds to indicate that they are still alert. It will be a few more years before you can shave your beard during the drive to work.

The self-steering car available today is a simple version of a much more complicated robotic beast called an unmanned ground vehicle (UGV). These advanced robots may look like regular cars (with a few extra antennae), or they may be flat and compact, with no pretense of providing a space for a useless human driver to sit and steer. A UGV uses a variety of sensors, such as stereo cameras, laser-range finders, and global positioning system (GPS) navigation to traverse city streets and backwoods

SELF-STEERING CAR CONSOLE

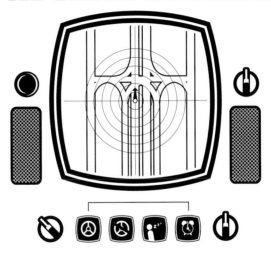

country without wrecking, getting lost, or killing any innocent human bystanders. UGV technology is progressing rapidly, spurred by the DARPA Grand Challenge competition, in which a two-million-dollar prize is awarded to the team that can design a car that can cross many miles of terrain in the shortest amount of time — without a human driver. The 2007 DARPA Grand Challenge will be a sixty-mile course in a mock-urban setting. With the recent boom in research, there are now hundreds of prototype UGVs, including golf carts, sedans, minivans, and (predictably) a full-sized military Humvee.

Unmanned ground vehicles have proven themselves in the great wide open, but problems remain to be solved before completely autonomous cars hit the city streets. Obstacles abound, but without a broad understanding of the world, a robot car cannot tell the difference between a harmless clump of grass and a farmers' market. *Negative obstacles*, such as holes in the ground, are particularly difficult for robot cars to identify. Navigation is also more difficult in cities, where tall buildings and bridges can block crucial GPS signals and soft, delicate targets (called pedestrians) abound. Thus, more-refined, city-dwelling UGVs are developing at a slower pace than their wild country cousins.

In the 2005 DARPA Grand Challenge, a robotic VW Touareg named "Stanley" completed the 132-mile off-road race (complete with tunnels and cliffs) in 6 hours and 53 minutes. The reward? Two million dollars.

Talking, self-steering cars are available for purchase right now. Yet you must resist the urge to throw down this book, don a black leather jacket, and devote your life to fighting crime with the help of an artificially intelligent smart car named KITT. Consumer-ready self-steering cars are only semi-autonomous — the real deal is yet to come. Fully autonomous unmanned ground vehicles are at the prototype stage, but you can look forward to an intelligent vehicle that can sense, think, and act more quickly than you can in complicated environments.

FLYING CAR

Look at your car sitting there in the driveway — sad, squat, all four tires on the pavement. You should feel sorry for your car for the same reason that you should feel sorry for yourself: You are both flightless. Optimistic drivers of the past imagined a future in which the stubby tail fins of their cars morphed into broad wings. According to the car companies at the World's Fair of 1939, your driveway was destined to become a runway, the highway a skyway, and the only speed limit the speed of sound.

The first attempts at creating flying cars were fairly simple — install an airplane engine and two wings on a regular car. The first attempts were also disastrous. Henry Ford's "sky flivver" flew in 1928, but production was nixed after an unlucky pilot died in a crash. In 1956, Moulton Taylor, an engineer who earlier had helped develop the cruise missile, unveiled the Aerocar. In default mode this "plane-mobile" could cruise on the highway at 65 mph, towing a tidy trailer that contained wings, tail, and propeller. Once the wings were attached, the little yellow Aerocar could leap from the highway at 55 mph and cruise up to 100 mph at around 12,000 feet with a range of up to 300 miles. After landing, you could park the car-plane in the garage (just remember to take off the wings first). The Aerocar worked fine conceptually, but it was too impractical for everyday use — a business deal for full-scale production

fell through in the early 1970s. The only remaining
Aerocar prototype was purchased by a fan who saw it
advertised in the classifieds.

> **In the pre-automobile days of the late nineteenth century, over 10,000 dead horses had to be removed from New York City streets every year.**

If you are averse to purchasing dangerous relics listed in
newspaper ads and you still want to acquire a flying
car, the solution may be to let NASA take care of it.
That's right, NASA gave us gooey foam pillows,
dehydrated ice cream, and those shiny space blankets,
and now it's about to fork over the flying car too. NASA
scientists working on the Small Aircraft Transportation
System (SATS) project made inroads on the two main
problems holding back personal air travel on a massive,
nationwide scale: midair collisions and complicated
piloting mechanisms.

NASA eschews the term "flying car," preferring
"personal air vehicle" instead. Nevertheless, NASA has
imagined and researched flying cars that would
humiliate George Jetson. Until their vehicle program was
eliminated in 2005, the folks at Langley Research Center
planned to roll out three prototypes in sequence: a
small, almost conventional prop plane that would tuck its
wings in on the highway (it shouldn't cost any more than
a Mercedes Benz); a two-seater with rear-propeller
drive; and, for tight parking spots, a car capable of

rising straight up into the air like a helicopter for a vertical takeoff. Merely providing the vehicles is not enough, however; if everyday people are to use them, scientists must know how to track thousands of these car-planes. And knowing is half the battle.

Collision-deterring navigation systems are key to transforming highways into skyways. Regular people just can't be trusted to avoid pasting themselves against office buildings. Instead, personal air vehicles will use GPS and cell phone technology to automatically broadcast information about location and speed to ground-based towers. From the ground, an automated computer system will update the flight path of every sky vehicle and provide instant directions — automatically avoiding collisions and minimizing flight time. Meanwhile, onboard sensors will detect nearby trees, buildings, and power lines and avoid collisions. And the jackpot bonus item for the sky-car consumer: For most of the flight the human "driver" can take care of anything besides flying, like eating a whole bag of potato chips.

At some point, however, the pilot-driver must be called on to steer. Recently, NASA scientists discovered that most people love to play video games but hate to die in fiery airplane crashes; they are capitalizing on this common sentiment by designing air vehicles that are controllable with simple video-game-like joysticks. Automatic collision-avoidance technology and self-correcting flight controls should allow just about anyone to master his or her own personal air vehicle — even Daryl, your slow cousin.

NASA prototypes may be exciting (and legitimate), but they aren't available to the public right this second. So turn your attention to the Moller M400 Skycar — a partially tested prototype offered in the 2005 Neiman Marcus gift catalog. Paul Moller, a former UC Davis engineering professor, has spent all of his money and more than forty years trying to build a flying car. The current model is a cherry-red coupe that looks as though it should be dogfighting TIE fighters outside the Death Star. The futuristic Skycar has four seats (carrying up to 750 pounds), a maximum air speed of 375 mph, and a range of about 750 miles. In theory, it gets more than 25 miles to the gallon. On the ground, the Skycar should travel a dinky 30 to 35 mph, just fast enough to get to an empty parking lot and stun everyone with a sweet vertical takeoff. Prototypes like the Skycar have been on the verge of full-scale production for almost a century, and it may be another hundred years before you can score that most badass symbol of the space age, the flying car.

WHERE'S MY JETPACK?

HOVERBOARD

Wide-eyed children of the eighties watched in astonishment as Michael J. Fox (a.k.a. Marty McFly) shredded pavement on a hovering skateboard in *Back to the Future Part II*. The hoverboard was just like a skateboard, but with one crucial difference: no wheels. His pink and teal board had "magnetic" pads on the bottom and with a quick push-off could silently cruise over grass, pavement, and even water. While this highly desirable piece of movie technology seems very plausible, it crushingly remains fiction. I think I speak for all of us when I say, "Thank you for breaking my heart, Michael J. Fox."

But dry your eyes, sport — hoverboards do exist, sort of. There are serious, but partially surmountable, technical challenges to making a piece of wood fly, especially over multiple surfaces, noiselessly, and without running out of energy within five minutes. These challenges have not stopped inventors from scheming, and there are several existing prototypes to choose from — none of which solve all of the problems at once.

Building your own hoverboard prototype is apparently easy. According to plans purchased from a back-page advertisement in a comic book, humankind's most state-of-the-art hoverboard can be built with parts harvested from a gas-powered leaf blower. Every *hovercraft* works on the same simple principle: Fans push air downward and the ground pushes the board up. Roughly, you'll need a motor from a leaf blower, a skateboard-sized hunk of plywood, and plenty of plastic and duct tape. These components form the three main pieces of a hoverboard: the engine, the board, and the rubber "skirt." Make a hole in the plywood board big enough for the leaf-blower nozzle. Now staple a sheet of plastic to the bottom of the board; this thin plastic skirt seals the area between the ground and the board, trapping the air and creating more lift. Finally, attach the leaf blower motor near the end of the board and fire it up. The whole contraption takes only a few hours to build and moves like a puck floating over an air hockey table.

TOP VIEW

Similar but more complicated hoverboards can be purchased from Future Horizons Inc. This company produces a variety of handmade or do-it-yourself hoverboard kits. These high-powered hoverboards are made of fiberglass shells and weigh about eighty pounds. Rear-mounted "thrusters" can push the board forward without your feet pushing off the ground. Another commercially available hovercraft, the Arbortech Industries Airboard, doesn't resemble a hoverboard at all, but may still be a lot of fun if you don't mind the expensive price tag. The disc-shaped Airboard is a gas-guzzling beast that stretches approximately six feet long and weighs over two hundred pounds. This self-powered hovercraft can move up to 15 mph over land or water.

As it stands, hovercraft technology would probably not be useful for escaping from angry hooligans in a quasi-futuristic park setting. Current prototypes are too heavy, noisy, and slow. They may be perfect for cruising over flat surfaces like water, ice, or a well-manicured lawn, but they are dangerously inept on city streets. The wheels of a regular skateboard provide a conduit for control between the leaning, swiveling, foot-pumping rider and the city streets. Without wheels to provide friction between ground and board, however, a hovercraft can't steer precisely, slow down or stop quickly, or regulate speed when it goes downhill. In a freestyle competition, the ordinary wooden skateboard wins for now.

Luckily, there exists another

BOTTOM VIEW

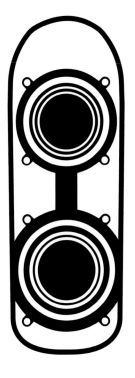

breed of "experimental" approach that capitalizes on ten-dollar words such as "antigravity," "ionic field," and "supermega atomic power pack." HoverTech offers the best of the worst from the fringe science community. The company promises a hoverboard that floats silently at up to a foot above the ground — without the use of fans, jets, or any moving parts. The key idea is to *ionize* a column of air (i.e., make the air electrically charged) and then surround it with a cylindrical magnetic field which prevents air from escaping from under the board — sort of like a super hovercraft with an impenetrable rubber skirt. In theory, trapping ionized air beneath a board is possible, but the key problem is power — there isn't any existing way to provide enough of it on a mobile platform. However, with enough juice a rider could stylishly scoot around on a foot-high column of trapped air.

Some crazy-ass mad science will have to go down before you can cruise around on Marty McFly's pink party board. In the meantime, hovercraft-based hoverboards are a reasonable real-world solution to humankind's critical hoverboard shortage. Personal hovercraft could become a common sight as engines shrink in size and grow in efficiency, and as fans become quieter and more powerful. So read a comic, send off your nickel in exchange for secret hoverboard instructions from the government, and hope that your dad doesn't notice that his leaf blower is missing.

TELEPORTATION

Why transport when you can teleport? In the classic *Star Trek* television series teleportation was commonplace from the deck of the USS *Enterprise*. The only danger was to nonessential actors, who were fated to be torn limb from limb by a papier-mâché moon beast upon being "beamed" to the surface. Now, brace yourself for a total brain meltdown: Teleportation is a real area of research and scientists are making solid progress with microscopic, inanimate objects.

In 1993 an international crack squad of scientists stood huddled in a secluded laboratory. All six physicists were men — five wore glasses, three were bald, and two had scary "math beards." Over the next few minutes, a machine employing an obscure law of quantum physics teleported a photon from one side of the room to the other. The scientists completed their mission, heralding a new era of research in teleportation. The preceding story is identical to the backstory of the video game *Doom* (minus the flesh-eating demons that come boiling from the teleporter), but it is also true; today physicists routinely conduct teleportation experiments.

The area of physics relevant to this study is called *quantum teleportation*, defined as the transmission and reconstruction over arbitrary distances of the state of a quantum system. The key idea is to find a way to collect all the information about the object to be teleported and then to use that information to make an identical copy in some other place (like the surface of an alien planet that looks suspiciously like West Hollywood). The teleported copy

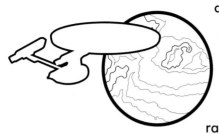 does not have to be made of the original parts and pieces — all that is necessary is the information about the original object and the raw material needed to reconstruct the object.

Unfortunately, it is fundamentally impossible to collect *all* the information about the object to be teleported. Quantum particles such as atoms and photons can exist in distinct states, like the head or tail of a coin. But they can also exist in a *superposition*, in several states at once, like a coin spinning in the air before it lands. Measuring the quantum system will force it into only one of these states, thereby losing the true state (or states). Thus, any attempt to collect information disturbs the quantum state of the particle (an outcome called the *projection postulate*). The only way around the projection postulate problem is to collect and transfer the information without ever learning what it is!

White-coated physicists use a clever jackknife of logic to "get her done" while respecting the laws of nature. *Entanglement* is a quantum property in which two particles become "entangled" so that the state of one is the opposite of the other — every single time and no matter how far apart the particles are. It is a creepy aspect of quantum physics (Einstein called it "spooky action at a distance"), but entanglement has been repeatedly verified, showing that a measurement on one particle can instantaneously influence the state of another particle at arbitrary distances. By cleverly entangling three particles it is possible to transfer information without collecting it.

Quantum teleportation via entanglement works like this: Let's say you have three particles called Alice, Bob, and Shaniqua. First entangle Alice and Bob so that they are in opposite states. Now entangle Bob and Shaniqua so that they are also opposites. Now we know that Alice and Shaniqua must be in the same state. The states never even have to be measured because the opposite of an opposite is the same thing — bam! Incidentally, Alice and Bob are destroyed during the entanglement process.

A delicious example involving quantum ice cream works best here. Imagine that each quantum particle either wants chocolate or vanilla ice cream. Now remember that if two particles are entangled, they will crave opposite flavors of ice cream. So let's say that the Alice particle wants chocolate. After entangling Alice with Bob, we know that Bob wants vanilla. If we entangle vanilla-loving Bob with Shaniqua, we know that Shaniqua must want chocolate ice cream — which is just what Alice wants. The same relationship holds no matter what flavor of ice cream Alice originally has a hankering for. (But don't think about it for too long or else you'll get an ice cream headache.)

A few interesting properties are revealed by this basic teleportation experiment. (Be careful, these revelations may blow your mind right out of your skull.) Remember how entangling two particles does not reveal

any information about the particles, aside from knowing that they are now opposites? This property of entanglement is crucial: Information from one particle is directly transferred to the other particle, which erases the state of the original particle and makes this teleportation and not cloning. (The original particle is not literally destroyed, but its information is erased and it becomes indistinguishable from its innumerable identical twins.) Furthermore, it is never necessary to know the location of Alice or Shaniqua — the entanglement property works anywhere and anytime without regard to location. During teleportation Shaniqua and Alice could be in the same room, or Shaniqua could be on a speeding spacecraft in deep space and Alice could be at a Denny's restaurant — on the moon!

The teleportation process will break down your original body and rebuild it someplace else, but you won't have to make any deep existential personal decisions about teleporting anytime soon. Quantum teleportation experiments abound, but so far have only been applied to elementary particles such as photons, trapped ions, and blobs of cesium gas. These particles are easier because they have very few quantum states (for example, an electron has up spin or down spin and a photon can be polarized vertically or horizontally). For more complicated particles (with more quantum states), teleportation techniques will have to advance considerably. To teleport a person, the machine would have to pinpoint and analyze all of the 10^{28} atoms in the human body. You could, however, do physicists a favor and lose some weight already.

UNDERWATER HOTEL

The Futurama II exhibit of the 1964 New York World's Fair predicted a sea-tastic future that featured undersea hotels with mammoth observation windows for studying sea life, minisubmarine excursions, and all the modern conveniences that we just can't live without — like oxygen, precious oxygen. These hotels were supposed to be clustered in heated little domed cities that rested snugly on the seafloor below gently lapping waves. Each dome city was to be connected by underwater submarine routes and seabed motorways with no speed limits. The Futurama exhibit was probably fatally optimistic, but behold — the mighty future has sort of arrived!

Human beings have spread to (and fought over) almost every corner of the planet, but nary a nation has laid claim to the "other" 70 percent of the planet. In the 1960s and 1970s, taming the sea was a pressing concern for the United States, Germany, France, the USSR, Great Britain, and the notoriously land-greedy Canadians. Manifest destiny had shoved humankind to the coasts, and for a brief time there was a race to colonize the open sea. Politicians envisioned citizens immigrating to the unlimited reaches of the ocean, riding sea tractors to harvest sprawling fields of nutritious seaweed and mining giant clams for treasured sea pearls. During this era more than sixty underwater habitats were constructed on seabeds all over the world. In these test-beds divers could stay submerged for a few days or weeks. The land under the sea was suddenly a very happening place, yet today only two underwater laboratories are left.

> **More people have traveled into outer space than have traveled to the deep ocean. Thus, if there were ever a brawl between astronauts and aquanauts, the astronauts would whoop ass.**

One of the most successful (and ultimately doomed) projects was run by the U.S. Navy. During the 1960s, the Sealab program was developed to further research sea colonization. Aquanauts found that life underwater is harsh, unlike the trip-fest described by the Beatles song "Yellow Submarine." Sea-bottom habitats are extremely dangerous (and expensive) due to darkness, pressure, and extreme cold. Nevertheless, the experimental underwater habitats furthered the science of deep-sea diving and rescue and helped scientists understand the psychological affects on humans who live in cramped isolation for extended periods of time. The Sealab

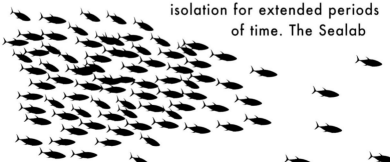

program ended in 1969 after a
fatal accident in the third and
final habitat, Sealab III.
(Allegedly, the habitat's air
supply was sabotaged,
and the culprit was
never caught.) These
days, underwater habitats are designed not for
military research, but for civilian relaxation.

So pack your flippers and prepare to relax,
because an underwater hotel exists and is open for
business. The Jules' Undersea Lodge is located just off
the coast of Key Largo, Florida, and about one
hundred feet underwater. The hotel began life in 1972
as a top-of-the-line underwater lab with the appetizing
name La Chalupa. These days, paying customers (for
a few hundred dollars per night) can hang out until
the money dries up. After a quick suit-up into diving
gear, guests can swim down to the air lock. The
laboratory-turned-hotel is shaped like a giant H and
stands on stubby legs that lift it off the seafloor. An
umbilical cord sends down a constant supply of fresh
air and water. Stay in and watch DVDs, look out the
42-inch round windows, or scuba dive as much as you
want (called *saturation diving*) — as long as you stay
underwater there won't be any decompression
sickness. Also, don't forget to bring your significant
other; you will want to join the "Five Fathom Club."
Remember that pets are not allowed, even if they
bring their own diving equipment.

Past guests report that staying at the only existing underwater hotel is suspiciously like sleeping in a sunken RV. However — according to a late-night commercial that I saw — underwater hotels of the glorious near future will not be hollowed out of old research labs. Several corporations are working toward building underwater luxury hotels in tropical destinations.

One such dream, called the Poseidon Undersea Resort, is a sunken luxury hotel off the coast of Eleuthera Island in the Bahamas. No need to bother putting on your scuba gear — the hotel will be accessible from the shore by a slow-cruising escalator. As in a submarine, the twenty-suite facility will be maintained at one atmosphere — the same as the surface. Guestrooms will have transparent acrylic bay windows equipped with outside lighting controls and fish feeders. The revolving restaurant will offer guests 360-degree views of a surrounding coral reef. Currently, investors are being corralled to pay for the forty-million-U.S.-dollar construction.

Finding investors is no problem in Dubai, one of the seven emirates of the oil-rich United Arab Emirates. The nation is undergoing a vast transformation, with ongoing architecture projects so numerous and fantastical that almost anything goes —

even the world's most ridiculous underwater hotel. Apparently named without irony, the Dives of the World experience in Dubai will boast a new underwater hotel with the proud name Hydropolis. Scuba diving trips are planned that will include inspecting sunken aircraft, ships, and even replica towers, pyramids, and Roman columns. The 220-suite facility is scheduled to open in late 2006. The cost to realize this wet dream is estimated at over half a billion U.S. dollars. If you've seen gas prices, however, you will know that the Dubai people are good for it. Thanks to entrepreneurship and oil money, your underwater honeymoon may be just a deep breath away.

DOLPHIN GUIDE

During the sea colonization craze of the 1960s it only stood to reason that humans would need powerful underwater allies. From watching reruns of the television show *Flipper* (1964–1968), scientists knew conclusively that the dolphin reigned as the most intelligent and helpful of all sea creatures. Over the years, these gentle cetaceans have appealed to humans of all sorts — hippies thought morally superior dolphins were choosing to live a transcendental experience, and soldiers were eager to teach the fish-eaters how to lay mines for food.

There are presently over forty species of dolphin living in oceans and rivers worldwide. The species that we most often see flouncing around water parks is called the bottlenose dolphin. These underwater mammals make likely companions for people; they are highly intelligent (some dolphin species can teach each other how to use tools) and descended from decent god-fearing, land-living mammals — just like us. Dolphins are also very social creatures; they live together in *pods* of up to a dozen animals. In special circumstances (like when Mum-Ra and his band of mutants are poised to destroy the Thundercats), dolphin pods will join forces to form unstoppable *superpods* composed of over a thousand dolphins. The social nature of dolphins can also have a dark side: Some captive dolphins seem to have committed suicide by self-battering or starvation — most notably one of the dolphins that played the original Flipper. (And you thought ol' Flipper went to go live on a farm in the country.)

To tame the mighty dolphin, we must first understand the inner workings of its mind, which is largely concerned with fish. In fact, the dolphin is a highly evolved fish-eating machine. Dolphins use two forms of communication to catch prey: a medley of whistles for interdolphin communication and a series of acoustic clicks used to locate food (called *echolocation*). Like wolves, dolphins work in teams to locate and corral their prey. Echolocation is a powerful hunting tool — dolphins can identify and close in on moving targets in murky water at up to two hundred feet. Essentially a high-tech form of the game Marco Polo, echolocation involves bouncing sound off of a target and then measuring how long it takes to return. Dolphins also have a terrifying superpower that would probably be called the *stun-scream* in a video game: they can deliver a powerful blast of low-frequency sound that incapacitates underwater prey. Between those wide innocent eyes, a dolphin has all the equipment necessary to act as the ultimate underwater guide.

When not performing backflips for drooling toddlers at Sea World, dolphins occasionally use their extreme dexterity for more sinister purposes — our gentle friends have been trained for underwater antics since the cold war era of the 1950s. The U.S. Navy routinely trains dolphins, sea lions, and beluga whales under the U.S. Navy Marine Mammal Program. Dolphins are outfitted with acoustic trackers or tethered cameras and sent into the briny deep to patrol for enemies, recover downed planes, or spot dangerous sea mines. Unlike human divers, dolphins have superior biological senses, can perform repeated long-duration deep dives, and lack a crippling fear of handling unexploded ordnance. It may be surprising, but the United States routinely deploys teams of highly trained military dolphins to foreign waters during wartime.

> **Bottlenose dolphins have been trained to "tag" enemy swimmers with a marker so they can be apprehended; however, the U.S. Navy steadfastly denies ever training a dolphin to attack a human.**

Convincing a dolphin to do your bidding for fun and profit is no easy task. Modern dolphin trainers persuade dolphins to play along by using good old *operant conditioning*. In this approach, every behavior of the dolphin is followed by a response from the trainer. Desired behavior is intermittently rewarded with either *primary reinforcement* (usually fish) or *secondary reinforcement* (such as a back rub). Because instant rewards are not always possible, a trainer will often whistle (called a *bridge*) when the dolphin is doing well. Undesired behavior is met with *nonreinforcement*, in which the trainer completely ignores the dolphin and may even leave the dock.

When dolphins are unhappy with trainers, they also employ nonreinforcement and sometimes swim away. The trainer must take care not to become the trained. (*Punishment* is not commonly used during training by dolphins or humans.) By all accounts, being a dolphin trainer is great; you get to work with the smartest mammal in the sea, and hey, all the buckets of fish you can eat.

But short of joining the military or the cast of the next *Flipper* movie, how can a regular person find a loyal underwater guide? What's more, how do you form a loving, lasting relationship with your dolphin in these turbulent times? First of all, there are no schools specifically designed for dolphin trainers — most people get started by working at zoos or aquariums. Secondly, love affairs between trainers and their dolphins do spring up occasionally. In the summer of 1965 a woman named Margaret Howe lived twenty-four hours a day for six days a week with a dolphin named Peter in a modified, flooded house. Designed by John Lilly, the house was normal, but with 24 inches of seawater added so that Peter could glide freely throughout. As the months passed, Margaret grew more lonely and depressed, although the dolphin arguably learned to speak "humanoid" by re-creating and using a few English words. Eventually, the dolphin started exhibiting courting behavior and a slightly scandalous relationship bloomed between the human-dolphin couple. Further proof that anyone who wasn't alive during the "anything-goes" period of the sixties really missed out.

Dolphins are our fellow mammals under the sea — whether you're seeking a love affair or an underwater assassin. As a uniquely adapted species (a dolphin has more sensory apparatus than you can shake a nuclear submarine at), the dolphin sets the precedent for cooperation between humankind and denizens of the sea. It is illegal to capture a wild dolphin, but many seaside resorts offer reasonably priced (and sometimes criminally unregulated) "swim-with-the-dolphins" programs. When the time comes to acquire a loyal underwater guide (and it will), leave your pathetic air-breathing Labrador at home — the dolphin is your best bet.

ENEMY

ENEMY MARKER

SPACE VACATION

Some days you just want to get away from it all and take off for somewhere remote — like deep space. Life's problems just seem smaller from several thousand million miles away. Luckily, ours is the first generation in which space vacations have become possible. The doors of the International Space Station swing wide for the ultra wealthy, and space venture capitalists are feverishly planning how to bank off of the common space tourist. So fill the ice chest with beer, smear yourself with SPF 1000, and stuff the kids in the trunk because it's time to go on a space vacation — in the flippin' future!

All you need for routine commercial space travel is a cost-effective, reusable launch vehicle. Airlines started making wild promises way back in 1968, when Pan Am began accepting reservations for moon flights. The list grew to more than 93,000 people, but the closest the airline company came to spaceflight was to have "Pan Am" written on the shuttle in Stanley Kubrick's movie *2001: A Space Odyssey*. In real life, NASA currently uses three space shuttles (the *Discovery, Endeavor*, and *Atlantis*) that are mostly reusable (the fifteen-story solid rocket boosters are recovered from the sea and refilled) but not very cost-effective. In 1996 the Ansari X PRIZE competition set out to change that.

To spur development of a reusable launch vehicle, the X PRIZE foundation offered ten million dollars to the team with the first vehicle to reach suborbital altitudes (about 70 miles high) twice in a row. There were twenty-six competitors with a variety of wild ideas on how to get the job done, and there was one winner, Burt Rutan, who designed SpaceShipOne. Small enough to fit in your garage, SpaceShipOne is made of a light hull of woven graphite attached to a rocket motor that runs on the chemical reaction between laughing gas and rubber. The vehicle reached space twice in two consecutive weeks in 2004 — leaving its two pilots weightless for a full four minutes each time. As it turns out, 70 miles is high enough to see the curvature of Earth and to feel weightlessness, two prime tourist selling points. It is no surprise that several space tourism companies emerged from the aftermath of the Ansari X PRIZE competition.

One such company, Virgin Galactic, promptly licensed SpaceShipOne for use in suborbital flights for tourists (tickets are already on sale for about a quarter million dollars apiece). The next version, SpaceShipTwo, will sweeten the profit margin by carrying up to five passengers along with two pilots. Meanwhile, the Aera company is piggybacking on the Florida Space Authority's Cape Canaveral site to launch its Altairis rocket, which takes off vertically with six passengers to the height of about 80 miles before landing like an airplane. There's even a new spaceport in the lush green fields of Oklahoma. The Oklahoma Spaceport (which used to be a Strategic Air Command base) will play host to the Rocketplane XP, a jet-and-rocket-powered four-seater that takes off and lands like a normal aircraft. Without question, the rush is on to haul tourists and their snot-nosed kids into space.

As such, yet another prize has emerged to help the space tourism industry lift off. America's Space Prize is a fifty-million-dollar award to anybody who can launch five people 250 miles up and orbit the planet twice before landing safely — and then do it again within sixty days. Not incidentally, 250 miles is the height necessary to ferry people to and from a real, working space hotel. The prize (which must be claimed by 2010) is a thinly veiled push by Bigelow Aerospace to spur development of the first space hotel.

You are not hallucinating as you read these wonderful words — space hotels have become a viable business interest. Bigelow Aerospace is currently brainstorming the design of an orbiting space hotel composed of inflatable modules. The design resembles a giant propane tank, except for the fact that it is *floating in space*. The company is serious enough to put fifty million dollars on the line, but anyone able to claim the prize must demonstrate the ability to dock with an inflatable space habitat. Americans seem to be on the verge of spending the weekend in orbit — if the U.S. government will allow it, that is.

Space-vacation development may suffer from the inescapable fact that in the United States the logical reaction to spilling hot coffee on yourself is to sue the coffee. Because coffee is not sentient, the next step is to sue the person who sold you the coffee. The final step is to clean the coffee off your scalded lap. This kind of logic understandably interferes with putting people into low Earth orbit and litigation issues are a serious impediment to space travel. In the United States, the Federal Aviation Administration (FAA) regulates the airline industry, but there is not yet a standard agency to regulate space travel. In 2004 the Commercial Space Launch Amendments Act introduced the concept of an informed-consent passenger liability waiver, but it was only a temporary solution. The FAA's Commercial Space Transportation Office is now producing a set of permanent guidelines for spaceflight operations. People are quick to sue when they slip and fall a few feet, so we must ask: What happens when a person slips and falls for a few hundred miles?

If you are brave enough to not care about little things like safety and litigation, then take off that Hawaiian shirt and put on your shiny silver spacesuit (you don't want to look like a space tourist). If you happen to be sitting on tens of millions of dollars, now is the time to call the Russian government and schedule a vacation in outer space. With a little more patience (and more time to save money), you can cut your fare to the bone and take a short suborbital flight. With a lot more patience and an undisclosed but surely insane amount of money, you can spend the week in a giant inflatable hotel in space. And isn't that what happiness is *really* all about?

WHERE'S MY JETPACK?

HOLOGRAM

When the grainy, three-dimensional image of Princess Leia from *Star Wars* implored Obi-Wan Kenobi for help, the entire world leaned forward and said, "I want that!" Later, we watched characters from *Star Trek: The Next Generation* as they constantly battled evil holograms-come-to-life from the holodeck. Science fiction loves holograms more than fat kids love cake, but so far holograms have not appeared often in our daily lives. Luckily, that may change soon — preliminary products are on the market and television's next evolutionary step is to go all three-dimensional.

A *hologram* is a three-dimensional image of an object that shows a different view from every angle — just like seeing the object in reality. Dennis Gabor won a Nobel Prize in Physics in 1971 for inventing *holography*, the science of producing holograms. The very first holograms were static images, like photographs. However, unlike conventional photographs, holograms contain extra information about the size, shape, brightness, and contrast of the object in the image. This information is stored when light is bent (*diffracted*) by interference fringes on the holographic surface. When new light hits a finished hologram, the information stored as an interference pattern re-creates the optical wavefront that was reflected off the original object. In a technical sense, seeing a true hologram is exactly the same as seeing the real object. The question is how long will it be before we see holograms in, on, and around our living room televisions.

Stop wishing for HDTV and start wishing for 3DTV. This

holy grail of holograms is largely responsible for the hologram research over the past few decades. It began in Japan in 1964, shortly after the Tokyo Olympic Games. The challenge was serious — to attain HDTV resolution with just sixteen different viewpoints requires updating around 33 million pixels at least 30 times per second. (In contrast, a high-end LCD panel television updates about 2 million pixels 60 times a second.) Now, more than forty years later, researchers at Mitsubishi Electric Research Laboratories (MERL) have finally developed an expensive prototype system that manages to do just that. The system uses sixteen synchronized cameras to capture multiple perspectives of a scene and sixteen projectors with *lenticular screens* (specially coated surfaces that reflect different images from different angles, like the hologram prizes in a Cracker Jack box). The system requires eight personal computers to run, and the viewpoint only changes horizontally, in an arc of 30 degrees. Another promising system belongs to the Spatial Imaging Group at MIT. The system, called the Mark-II Holographic Video Display, uses acoustic modulators, beam splitters, moving mirrors, and lenses to create interactive holograms. Unfortunately, the display hardware is much larger than the actual displayed image and the system cannot record and play back in real time. For now, the closest approximation to 3DTV is apparently only available to hardworking graduate students.

Although 3DTV won't be available to the consumer for a while, other holographic techniques abound. Human beings use a variety of visual clues to pick up on three-dimensional information. Two of the most important cues are called *binocular parallax* and *motion parallax*. Binocular parallax occurs when you see a slightly different image of the same object from each eye (because of the space your nose takes up). Motion parallax occurs when, as you are in motion, objects that are closer appear to move across your field of view more quickly than objects that are farther away. For example, when you look out the window of a car, the nearby trees may seem to race by while distant mountains hardly move. Researchers are exploiting these visual cues to make holograms a reality.

In the past, three-dimensional displays using binocular parallax required viewers to wear plastic glasses with special lenses; two separate images were projected at the same time — each lens allowed only one image to enter each eye. Newer 3-D video displays sidestep the glasses by interweaving multiple images in vertical stripes. Each stripe is meant for only one eye and special coatings built into the screens send the images to the correct eye. The drawback of these lenticular screens is that they put a strain on the eyes and brain of the viewer, causing headaches, dizziness, and nausea. Clearly, this problem must be solved before 3DTV debuts — people won't tolerate missing the on-screen action due to "barf breaks."

Commercially available holographic displays *do* exist. Although not technically holograms, these devices project two-dimensional images into thin air. IO2 Technology offers the Heliodisplay, which modifies air temperature to project a floating two-dimensional video screen. If you thought a flat-panel monitor was thin, wait until you see a no-panel,

42-inch touch-screen monitor that hovers two feet above your desk! Similarly, FogScreen Inc. produces a projection screen that you can walk through. The device uses ordinary tap water to create a dry-feeling, invisible wall of fog that reflects projected video from any standard source. The device can be used to create walk-through walls, virtual billboards, or a television screen that pops up from the middle of the room.

Advertisers are also increasingly employing holography. More and more, they are interested in posters that, rather than stay put on a wall, appear to hang just out of reach. Researchers at Color Holographics are manufacturing giant poster-holograms by coating a piece of glass (or Plexiglas) with a chemical that is reactive to laser light. Typically, eighty separate frames of 35 millimeter film are put together to form three seconds of motion. The final poster looks like a window with a three-dimensional object trapped inside. During a recent deployment on a street, it was not uncommon for shoppers to dodge the empty air in which terrifying products seemed to float.

The first place to look for holograms will be in advertisements and entertainment venues. Certain consumer product conferences also play host to advanced prototypes, so get out and mingle with the nerd herd. Meanwhile, entrepreneurs are well aware that holography could revolutionize media and they are eager to profit from it. As long as there is money to be made, progress in holography will continue. In the meantime, you will have to settle for watching reruns of *Lost in Space* on a ten-foot square wall of future fog.

MOON SPACE
AVAILABLE

WHERE'S
MY JETPACK?

SMELL-O-VISION

In the sad world in which we live, the only smell that most TVs can produce is the smell of burning plastic. In the 1932 book *Brave New World*, Aldous Huxley imagined a future in which we — the shuffling masses — enjoyed going to full-sensory movies called "feelies." It seemed so plausible; the booming early movie industry looked as though it might gallop beyond vision and sound and into — you guessed it — nostril country. Yet no matter how hard you search a DVD's special features, you will not find a "smell track." The reason is simple: Our forebearers were given Smell-O-Vision and they turned up their noses.

Every time you smell something horrible (or something wonderful), it is because molecules from the thing you are smelling made it into your nose. Smelly objects are *volatile*, meaning that molecules (called *odorants*) are constantly evaporating from their surface and into the air. Baked bread is very volatile, while a slab of steel is nonvolatile. Inside your nose at the top of your nasal passages is a postage-stamp-sized patch of special neurons called *olfactory receptors*. These neurons have hairlike projections (called *cilia*) that directly bind with floating odor molecules. If your life is going well, this is the only part of your brain that is ever exposed directly to the atmosphere. A different olfactory receptor exists for each molecule that you can smell, and these receptors are coded into your genes and stored in your DNA. The average person can recognize 10,000 distinct smells. Over the years, people have tried many approaches to transform an understanding of smell into profit.

During the movie craze of the 1950s, a Swiss professor of *osmics* (the study of smells) named Hans Laube created Smell-O-Vision. Thanks to the help of investor Mike Todd Jr., the revolutionary technique was introduced to the noses of moviegoers in the 1960 film *Scent of Mystery*. A central "smell brain" (located in the projector room) pumped out thirty different smells, including flowers, garlic, pipe smoke, baked bread, coffee, oranges, shoe-shine wax, and the perfume of the mystery girl in the film. Smells were dispersed through more than a mile of tiny tubes hidden under seats throughout the theater. Back at the "smell brain," each scent was held in a small bottle on a rotating drum and blasts of odor were triggered by certain scenes of the movie. (Moviegoers with a good sense of smell could even solve the mystery.) The system worked surprisingly well, and twenty Smell-O-Visions were ordered, but fickle audiences preferred to watch movies and not to smell them. *Scent of Mystery* was yanked and rereleased under a new name without a trace of stink.

But wait — there was competition for last place. An inferior approach appeared in theaters a scant few weeks before *Scent of Mystery*. A documentary called *Behind the Great Wall* incorporated the AromaRama system, which pumped nightclub smoke and Asian spices through the theater's regular ventilation system. The AromaRama smells were indistinct, delayed, and proved difficult to clean out of the air-conditioning systems after movie showings. Neither Smell-O-Vision nor AromaRama caught on, but for the record, AromaRama was the greater failure.

A brief smell revival occurred in 1981, when John Waters paid homage to Smell-O-Vision by handing out scratch-'n'-sniff "Odorama" cards for the movie *Polyester*. Trusting moviegoers were met with a variety of surprise smells, including dirty socks.

In the intervening period, smelly technology has mostly stalled. One bankrupt company called DigiScents grabbed the market by the horns in 2000 and put out the iSmell device. (That's right, they named it that on purpose.) The small, plastic device generated odors by blending different "scent primaries." A collection of scent cartridges was heated in combination and the resulting smells pushed out by fan. A similar device is being tested in Tokyo theaters on the 2006 movie *The New World*. Instead of synchronizing scents to movie scenes, the computerized fragrances will act as subtle "mood enhancers." Meanwhile, a Japanese firm called K-Opticom is prototyping Kaori Web — a device for providing smell-enhanced Web sites. You'll know that you have reached the right Web site when you smell Astroglide.

In the middle of the last century the public was given a magical, powerful gift: Smell-O-Vision. If moviegoers had reacted differently, the wonder of Smell-O-Vision might be commonplace today. Unfortunately, the idea never caught on and it continues to bankrupt new investors to this day. And that's why our theaters don't have nose tubes, our Web sites don't have iSmell, and this book doesn't have just the faintest odor of jasmine and gasoline.

ROBOT PET

It is an indisputable scientific fact that robots are awesome and totally sweet too. Human beings have long imagined using robots as workers, explorers, and servants, but we see them most often in the form of remote-controlled toys. Every kid knows, however, that the ultimate robot toy does not have a remote control — it is a pet with a mind of its own. While robo-pets have always been common in cartoons — from Dynomutt, Dog Wonder of *The Scooby-Doo/Dynomutt Hour* (1976), to Goddard, the robotic pup in *Jimmy Neutron: Boy Genius* (2001) — only recently have real robot toys evolved into full-fledged pets with emotions and needs.

Today's toy store shelves are crawling with robotic pets. Arguably, it all began with the Furby. This pint-sized robotic misfit was almost completely useless — just like a real pet. The original Furby could not move; it could only make noises and wiggle its ears, eyes, and eyelids. A Furby also could not learn; it came with a preprogrammed set of words and behaviors that were released over time to simulate learning. Owners who interacted with the Furby were rewarded with an unpredictable, immobile, testy little bird-thing with an attitude. Nevertheless, over 40 million Furbies were sold and a new version with speech recognition will soon be released. The market for robotic toys — even rudimentary ones — is huge.

Newer robot pets are already capable of simple locomotion. The remote-controlled RoboSapien V2 by

WowWee toys was designed by a NASA roboticist, not a toy maker. Although Robo's level of autonomy is minimal (it can wander aimlessly for up to five minutes), its range of physical abilities is impressive: The two-foot-tall RoboSapien can walk, dance, karate chop, and pick up and throw objects. It is also capable of making (mostly offensive) noises and of listening for and responding to loud noises. Meanwhile, the Roboraptor (RoboSapien's carnivorous cousin) can stalk the premises awkwardly and snap at your fingers with its plastic teeth.

But consumer toys of the near future are starting to really get fun. The makers of Furby have created a new creature — a cute, long-necked robotic sauropod the size of a kitten, named Pleo. Pleo is designed to mimic a friendly real-life pet dinosaur, if there were such a thing. Pleo can walk, wiggle, and nibble; and it moves smoothly in an organic, lifelike fashion via fourteen motors. Using a bit of artificial intelligence and information constantly collected from thirty-eight sensors, Pleo exhibits simulated emotions and has its very own personality — Pleo's sensory system and behavior model evolve over time based on its interactions with the world. Robotic pets can come in a no-holds-barred variety of shapes, and Pleo is only the first of many exotic robot pets.

Meanwhile, the rich can buy robotic pets that are smarter than toy store varieties and vastly more expensive. The discontinued Sony AIBO (Japanese for "companion") is a robotic dog about the size of a guinea pig. The AIBO uses high-end cameras and microphones to recognize human faces, understand speech, and follow verbal commands. It can walk, sit, and clamber over obstacles using all four legs. With the right software, an AIBO will

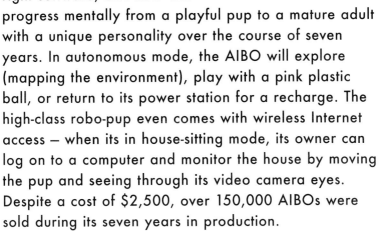

progress mentally from a playful pup to a mature adult with a unique personality over the course of seven years. In autonomous mode, the AIBO will explore (mapping the environment), play with a pink plastic ball, or return to its power station for a recharge. The high-class robo-pup even comes with wireless Internet access — when its in house-sitting mode, its owner can log on to a computer and monitor the house by moving the pup and seeing through its video camera eyes. Despite a cost of $2,500, over 150,000 AIBOs were sold during its seven years in production.

Although plenty of high-end and consumer-ready robotic pets are available now, the most radical pets exist in prototype form. Future robotic pets are designed to do more than just look cute and pee on the rug. The ridiculously adorable Paro robot (developed by Japan's National Institute of Advanced Industrial Science and Technology) looks like a baby harp seal and is designed to socialize with elderly nursing home residents. Paro is irresistible, with soulful black eyes and white, hypoallergenic fur. The robotic seal cannot walk, but will squeak and wiggle its flippers when it wants to be picked up. However, Paro is not all cuteness and sunshine — when humans cradle Paro, the robot can quietly monitor their health by sensing their heart rate and other physiological signs.

Playing with robo-puppies may be more fun than shaving a monkey, but we are only just learning about how interactions with realistic toy robots will affect adults — and children. Researchers at the University of Washington studied the reactions of preschool-age children to the Sony AIBO robotic dog and found that most (but not all) of the children understood that the robot is not "real." Even so, most children treated the robot as though it were a dog — simply because it emulates a real dog. Robotic pets are the forerunners of a new, morally ambiguous future populated by both humans and robots. The rules of interaction are not yet written, so think twice before you kick your child's whimpering robotic dog.

Whether they psychologically impact human children or not, robotic pets are likely to be a staple of futuristic entertainment. The fun is only compounded when robot pets come home to live with real pets, or when you have a gaggle of robotic dogs yapping at each other interminably. Robot pets are dropping in price and climbing the walls. The future is sure to be a glorious place where it is fine to live in a studio apartment with forty-two cats, as long as you can pay the electric bill.

SUPERHUMAN
ABILITIES

MIND-READING DEVICE

She loves me, she loves me not. Why not throw away those flower petals, peel back her forehead, and go directly to the source? The human skull isn't as thick as it once was. Current technology can bridge the gap between mind and reality, between thought and action, between Kant and Descartes. Modern *mind reading* is simply a matter of collecting and interpreting the electrical activity that courses through the human brain.

Let's start out simply: Humans constantly use external signals to read others' minds. Toward this end, much research is directed at using clever information to spot liars. The current standard is a *polygraph test*, which is known to have abysmal accuracy rates — somewhere at or below 50 percent. A polygraph also requires strapping elastic straps around a person (to measure breathing rate), placing blood-pressure cuffs on their arm (to measure heartbeat), and putting electrodes on their fingertips (to measure conductivity caused by perspiration). What a hassle. The U.S. Department of Homeland Security is now developing camera-based systems that read facial features and body language in its goal to spot liars. The system registers "micro-expressions" and "micro-gestures" that may be imperceptible to humans. These reactions are hard to regulate and fairly similar across race, gender, and culture. Better start practicing your poker face.

Or not. Researchers at the Mayo Clinic are developing an advanced polygraph test that doesn't stop at the skin's surface. An infrared camera can track the heat of blood flow through the smallest vessels of the human face. Preliminary research has uncovered a distinctive blood-flow pattern when someone is lying, with blood surging to the eye area — probably caused by a fight-or-flight response. Researchers dubbed this ghostly infrared camera image the "face of fear." People can learn to modify their respiration, perspiration, and even their heart rate — but it's next to impossible to avoid the face of fear. If you come home late from work again and your wife is wearing infrared goggles and a frown, expect a long night.

> **An exposed human brain has the consistency of room-temperature butter.**

You may wish that, like a stage performer with a thick unibrow, you too could read other peoples' minds. Well it isn't all that hard — with the right machinery. The human brain emits electrical activity as 100 billion *neurons* communicate and operate. Two varieties of mind-reading machines can eavesdrop on these mind-currents: invasive (a *subdural* electrode directly on your brain, called a *neural implant*) and noninvasive (a sticky patch containing an electrode on your forehead, called a *brain-computer interface*). After the brain signals are collected, a computer program (not a stage performer) analyzes and attaches meaning to them. However, instead of learning your deepest, darkest secrets, most computer-controlled mind readers are designed to help people with physical disabilities by converting thoughts into commands that can potentially control items as diverse as a computer cursor, a prosthetic limb, or the floodgates of the Hoover Dam.

So there you are, lying on your back with your head shaved, about to undergo minor brain surgery in order to control that massive robot arm that you've always wanted. This isn't going to hurt — really. The brain itself has no pain receptors — the pain fibers are entirely in the *dura mater* and other external coverings, all of which are nicely anesthetized. Thus, the surgery will be performed while you are awake and conscious. Your only discomfort will likely be neck pain caused by holding your head in one position for a long time. A tiny silicon chip (about the size of a baby aspirin) will be placed on the surface of your brain called the *motor cortex* — a strip that runs just above and in front of your ears. A matrix of hair-thin wires will penetrate your brain and begin listening to your brain waves. (Each "wire" is actually a small spike with a minuscule golden electrode.) The sensor will communicate with a dime-sized *pedestal*, a Matrix-style plug-in attached to your scalp. After a quick incision, you'll be stitched up, they'll fasten a few titanium screws, and you'll be ready to enjoy your new life as a superhuman man-machine.

A company called Cyberkinetics has already performed some of the first human trials, establishing an interface between the human cortex and a computer. Implanted patients who were previously "locked in" (completely unable to move but mentally sound) were able to move a cursor around a computer screen — their only interaction with the world. The BrainGate system goes one step further, allowing a paralyzed person to control a rubbery, disembodied artificial hand by brain power alone. Cyberkinetics also offers a neural monitoring product that can be used for up to thirty days to record and monitor brain activity. The ultimate goal is a wireless, unobtrusive system that enables those with severe motor impairments to control any available devices by thought alone. Too bad the initial medical trials are open only to those with severe impairment and not to the incurably lazy.

Let's not forget about the cyborg monkeys. In one experiment at the University of Pittsburgh, a test monkey was able to retrieve bananas by controlling a prosthetic arm with good old-fashioned monkey-thought. The system works like this: A sensor in the monkey's brain collects electrical signals from the motor cortex and a computer program interprets the signals and sends the appropriate command to a mechanical arm, which the monkey can see. (The monkey's real arm is strapped to its side, so there is no need to call in an expensive monkey-arm-amputation service.) The feedback loop has an imperceptible delay of only twenty milliseconds. For humans, however, controlling a robot arm in three dimensions is a difficult task: The human brain probably uses hundreds of millions of neurons for this, but the computer can only listen to a relative few. Current prototypes can control simple artificial limbs, but controlling complicated limbs like Dr. Octopus's metallic tentacles from *Spider-Man 2* is much more difficult.

Sure, people love to cram bundles of wires into the back of their heads, but isn't there an alternative? Another class of "intimate interfaces" can listen to your thoughts from outside the skin by paying attention to *biosignals*, such as *isometric* muscular activity generated from small or imperceptible movements (like breathing, tongue movements, or even thinking about making a movement). However, the most common brain-computer interface reads electroencephalogram (EEG) signals (brain wave activity) from an electrode-studded skullcap to figure out which parts of the brain are generating electrical activity. A team of Austrian researchers taught a quadriplegic patient to open and close a prosthetic hand in this manner, but the patient required five months of training. Cutting-edge techniques use artificial intelligence algorithms to reduce training times by helping the computer figure out what the user is trying to do. So far, these interfaces have been used as sort of a secret TV remote, but in the future they could be used to control cell phones, personal digital assistants (PDA)s, or even automobiles.

A new crop of advanced devices is allowing humans (and cyborg chimps) to harness the mysterious power of mental concentration. The conduit between brain and reality has always been the body, but bio-implantable neurosensors are cutting out the middleman and helping people — paralyzed or not — lay hands on the world directly from the mind. Someday soon you could have your ass scratched by a robot arm before you've even finished thinking about doing it — and that's worth every single monkey trial.

ANTI-SLEEPING PILL

In the land of the future we are all going to live forever, so there will be no time for sleep. For those of us who want to skip our solid eight, the solution is already here and, as usual, it is in pill form. The U.S. military is hell-bent on creating an army of metabolically enhanced supersoldiers with nerves of steel and bloodshot eyes. The same advanced technology that will allow an army of zombie soldiers to stalk the battlefield will allow you to finally watch the entire *Sopranos* series nonstop.

Anti-sleeping pills have a very practical application for people suffering from narcolepsy, an affliction that causes people to instantly fall asleep (usually as the punch line of a joke). To battle the cheap jokes, a French firm has developed a drug sold in the United States under the name Provigil (and Alertec in Canada). The active ingredient, called *modafinil*, was approved by the FDA in 1998 and is officially used to treat excessive sleepiness and to help cocaine addicts kick their habit. The U.S. Air Force has also tested modafinil on fighter pilots, instead of giving them the usual amphetamines that long-haired truck drivers have been using for decades. This wonder drug is set to banish sleep forever.

In trials, Provigil has been shown to successfully keep people awake for up to eighty-eight hours with negligible side effects and little risk of addiction. Unlike amphetamines, which stimulate the entire nervous system, modafinil simply shuts off the feeling of drowsiness. It may sound great, but calm down, ace; there is none of the euphoria induced by stimulants like cocaine or ecstasy. Modafinil keeps you awake and alert, but it doesn't prevent you from getting bored.

> **Federal legislation requires U.S. truck drivers to rest for at least 12 hours in a 24-hour period. Taking the weekend off is also mandatory (partying hard is optional, but recommended).**

ALERT SOLIDER USING ANTI-SLEEPING PILLS

Of course, nobody understands exactly how modafinil really works. One key discovery, however, is that the urge to fall asleep and the urge to wake up may be independent of each other. There is a reason that we wake up five minutes before the alarm goes off — humans are each outfitted with a biological "master clock." In 1972, scientists identified the biological clock portion of the brain, called the *suprachias-matic nucleus* (SCN). The SCN controls your circadian rhythm and is located in the hypothalamus, deep in your forehead behind the optical cortex. In one study, a group of squirrel monkeys had the SCN portion of their brains removed (*ablated*) and were found to sleep excessively (a condition called *hypersomnia*). It appears that the SCN does not cause sleepiness, but rather wakefulness — and without the SCN you can't fight the urge to sleep. Modafinil precisely targets and stimulates the SCN; otherwise, as the day wears on, the SCN will reduce the urge to stay awake until the impulse to sleep becomes nearly impossible to resist — and that's when your car plunges off the side of the road.

The FDA has only approved the use of modafinil to treat narcolepsy, obstructive sleep apnea, and shift-work sleep disorder, but regular folks with lesser sleep problems may soon be able to get their fix as well. The drug is expected to attract a wide market, including truckers, students, or anyone pulling an all-nighter. The drugmaker is optimistic, as no serious side effects of modafinil have been identified, however, sleep researchers urge caution — there is evidence that a lack of sleep hurts the endocrine and immune systems.

WEARY SOLIDER WITHOUT ANTI-SLEEPING PILLS

Although modafinil is readily available, research continues on creating a sleepless supersoldier. The DARPA "metabolic dominance" program is currently funding a study of the natural alertness mechanisms that allow the white-crowned sparrow to stay awake for up to two weeks during migration. Sleep deprivation is unavoidable during combat, and the goal is to produce a GI who can go without sleep for seven days by fine-tuning his or her metabolism on demand. The metabolically dominant soldier will be in peak physical and cognitive condition for three to five days, twenty-four hours a day (no sleep) and won't need calories (no food). Just think of the ridiculous dance parties this research will make possible. In the meantime, somebody please give DARPA a few battle droids so that its soldiers can get some rest.

If you can't get a legal prescription for modafinil, just stick to the world's most widely used stay-awake drug: caffeine. It works in a pinch, and anyway, people are far more likely to crave sleep than to avoid it — an estimated two thirds of Americans don't get enough sleep. Anti-sleep drugs may contribute more to our vision of a space-age future, but tranquilizers — called *hypnotics* by sleep doctors — potentially affect more people. Insomniacs outnumber those who crave painless all-nighters, so look for improvements in hypnotics before anti-sleeping pills proliferate.

INVISIBLE CAMOUFLAGE

In 1897, H. G. Wells imagined a hellish existence for a young scientist who managed to find the key to invisibility but not how to reverse it. More recently, in the movie *Predator* a big green extraterrestrial hunts humans while concealed in blurry, almost invisible battle armor. Harry Potter goes even further, disappearing completely beneath his wizard's cloak. Now the invisibility technology once reserved for sci-fi mags, movie theaters, and comic books is quietly sneaking up on us.

While hiding from your little brother is fun, the ability to hide from bullets can save your life. To that end, *adaptive camouflage* for personnel and vehicles has become a military priority. Traditional camouflage — common to the animal kingdom — uses a static color and shape pattern to blend in visually with the background. Researchers at NASA's Jet Propulsion Laboratory have defined adaptive camouflage as a form of camouflage that actively changes to best match the environment. The key idea is to wrap yourself in real-time images of the surrounding environment — sort of like wearing a flexible television screen.

You can get started right now: Aim a webcam backward over your shoulder and stand behind the computer monitor. Because the computer screen is displaying an image of what's behind you, anyone standing directly in front of you will see a rectangular hole where your totally ripped abs should be. Then imagine crouching inside a box made of flat-panel monitors with cameras pointing in every direction. Now imagine the U.S. military imagining a tank inside that box. The basic idea is sound, but don't sneak into the womens' locker room quite yet — the edges of the computer monitor are still visible and each view looks convincing from only one perspective.

Researchers from Tokyo University in Japan have developed an early prototype of adaptive camouflage. Their approach is simple: A video camera on the back of a white rain jacket collects an image that is projected onto the front of the jacket as if it were a movie screen. The jacket is made of a *retroreflective* material that clearly shows the projected image. Although casually glancing at the jacket reveals a ghostly image of whatever is behind it, this approach is little more than a parlor trick; it requires a separate projector and only works from front-on.

The real problem is to make adaptive camouflage show the right image from every angle at once, not just from the front. This is a challenge, but it isn't impossible. Remember those cheap holographic stickers — the ones that show a different image depending on how much they are tilted? Using a similar principle, it is theoretically possible to go invisible. First, the system needs at least six stereoscopic pairs of cameras (that's twelve in all) and they must be pointed in every direction. This will capture a complete image of the surroundings. Second, a dense array of display elements is needed, each capable of aiming light beams on their own individual trajectories. The refresh rate must be faster than the human eye in order to avoid creating a flickering effect. Anyone who plays video games knows that a high frame rate is tough to maintain when there is a lot of motion; the entire screen must refresh quickly without blurring, ghosting, smearing, or juddering. Finally, a hardworkin' wearable computer has to calculate the virtual scene to send to each element of the display. All the above technology then has to be stitched together into a wacky robe covered with moons and stars.

Invisibility applications extend past the battlefield and beyond the womens' locker room: Surgeons could see through their own fingers during operations, pilots could orient themselves by seeing through the airplane floor, and you could finally get a decent window in your basement apartment. Unfortunately, current technology only works at short distances, in dim places, and at select viewing angles. The only way to transcend these boundaries is to develop faster processors, brighter LEDs, and more-flexible display elements. Alternately, you could join a team of battle-hardened jungle commandos and track down and capture a *Predator* alien, being sure to remove its quasi-invisible battle gear before it has a chance to self-destruct.

ARTIFICIAL GILLS

A goldfish is arguably the most boring pet ever — only slightly more boring than sea monkeys. Yet a simple goldfish can plumb the mysteries of the briny deep while we humans flounder on dry land. Are you going to take that from a goldfish? The time has come to don a bright orange spandex suit and join Aquaman for a lifetime of underwater adventure! But beware: Starting life anew below the sea will only last about three and a half minutes unless you have the proper equipment — like a set of surgically attached gills.

Historically, humankind's underwater escapades have been strictly BYOO (bring your own oxygen). For centuries, *free divers* have been exploring the sea between deep breaths (the deepest recorded free dive was about 400 feet). In the fourth century B.C., Aristotle described the *diving bell*, a weighted bell-shaped container full of air. And by the nineteenth century, Europeans were wearing bulky *diving suits* with air hoses snaking up to the surface. Encased in these hose-fed monstrosities, brave mariners clambered around the bottom of the sea like ancient astronauts, wearing pressurized suits of solid metal. As time passed, diving suits became more high-tech, including features like claws, huge barrel joints, and interior seats. Even romantic diving suits built for two became available. By the twentieth century, advanced technology finally snipped the umbilical cord to the surface entirely.

The modern age of diving arrived in 1943, when Captain Jacques Cousteau and Emile Gagnan prototyped the *aqualung* — the first self-contained underwater breathing apparatus (SCUBA). Essentially, a scuba diver carries down a bag full of air. The trick is to fill the a cylindrical metal tank with around thirty pounds of compressed air — enough for about an hour. The air within the cylinder is compressed to 3,000 pounds per square inch, a hundred times the pressure of a car tire. Alas, breathing air at that pressure would pop your delicate lungs like festive party balloons. Therefore, the key contribution of the aqualung was the *regulator* — a two-stage device that instantly and safely reduces tank pressure, delivering a sip of air whenever a diver takes a breath. These days scuba diving is a common leisure activity, but it is hardly the most advanced way to swim with the fishes.

It is easy to spot a scuba diver — just look for all the bubbles. Traditional *open-circuit* scuba divers waste the vast majority of compressed oxygen that they carry. Human lungs do not absorb oxygen perfectly, and when a diver exhales, a good amount of precious oxygen (and not-so-precious carbon dioxide) bubbles back to the surface. On the other hand, a *fully closed-circuit* scuba (a type of *rebreather*) recycles exhaled air, getting rid of the carbon dioxide and returning extra oxygen to the tank. The result is a streamlined breathing system that produces no bubbles and lasts for hours on a small tank of oxygen. Be careful, rebreathers are only safe as long as they can "scrub" out poisonous carbon dioxide, and they may become saturated before you run out of oxygen.

Rebreathers maximize oxygen use, but an observant person may have noticed that fish rarely use tiny scuba tanks; on the contrary, fish rely on frilly red gills. Oxygen permeates most of the ocean, especially near the water's surface, where wind, waves, and currents pull air down from the atmosphere. Fish breathe by drinking — water enters the mouth and filters through the gill area, flowing past sheetlike *filaments* that are covered with red, spongy *lamellae*. These specialized organs filter oxygen from the water to keep our cold-blooded friends alive. Thus, drawing inspiration from fish, scientists have begun developing *artificial gills*.

> **Mice submerged in oxygen-rich water have been able to survive for up to a day.**

With the use of artificial gills, you may soon be able to breathe underwater as easily as a delicious bass. It is simple to construct a crude artificial gill (although not the surgically attached variety): Just take a watertight box and replace one wall with a *gas-permeable membrane* — like a sheet of silicone. The submerged box will stay filled with air (mostly oxygen and nitrogen) even if oxygen levels inside the box drop and carbon dioxide levels increase (which is what happens when someone decides to breathe). The simple design really works; Walter Robb (the inventor of highly permeable silicone) used such a box to support a submerged hamster for as long as fresh water flowed past the membrane to supply new oxygen. Unfortunately, this breakthrough never led to an underwater hamster ball.

Unless you have tiny hamster-lungs, artificial gill prototypes are not quite ready to use. The problem is that human beings consume too much oxygen for a portable system to keep up. The less efficient an artificial gill is, the more water it must process to retrieve oxygen. An early Prototype from Fuji Systems (called the Donkey III) kept a diver alive for a thirty-minute demonstration in 2002. The Donkey III is a box the size of a refrigerator that pumps water through oxygen-harvesting membranes. Aside from being unwieldy, the machine only maintained oxygen levels at a brain muddling 16 percent (normal air is 21 percent oxygen). Meanwhile, the Infoscitex company is developing a *biomimetic* silicon-based polymer membrane mask that closely imitates fish gills. Instead of a massive pump, the artificial gills will have a fractal microscopic structural form that maximizes surface area and access to oxygen.

Other researchers are ignoring the talents of fish altogether and applying good old hard-core physics. The *aquagill* consists of a cylindrical tank containing a rapidly spinning centrifuge; the device spins water to the outside of the cylinder, leaving a vacuum in the middle that pulls in air from the surrounding water. The challenge is to process enough water to keep a diver alive, which means a big water pump and enough batteries to power it. Due to these limitations, this technology will probably be used to supply oxygen to underwater habitats and not individual divers.

There is another creature of the deep that does not require scuba tanks — the nuclear submarine. With access to a nuclear reactor, these monsters can electrocute the air out of water. *Electrolysis* refers to a method used to separate unwanted leg hair from women *and* a method used to separate oxygen from water. We call water H_2O for a reason: Each molecule is made of two hydrogen atoms and one oxygen atom. Passing a powerful electric current through water will blast the liquid into hydrogen and oxygen gas. Pure water is a poor conductor, so a liquid called an *electrolyte* is added before the Tasering begins. The process requires a lot of energy, so until portable atomic backpacks are available, divers will have to find oxygen elsewhere.

As we have seen, oxygen is getting easier to come by under the sea, but the pressure of living life underwater is still high. High pressure at around thirty feet below causes nitrogen gas to collect in the blood. This can quickly cause *nitrogen narcosis* (sensuously referred to as the "rapture of the deep"), which can cause a diver to become suicidally disoriented. On the other hand, if the diver ascends too quickly, the dissolved nitrogen will suddenly convert back into air, sending nitrogen bubbles throughout the body that can destroy joints, damage cartilage, and block capillaries in the brain. Worse yet, pure oxygen becomes toxic at depths of more than thirty feet. Straying below that depth requires a mixed-gas rebreather, which delivers exotic gas mixtures (and only a sip of oxygen). Arrr, the sea is indeed a harsh mistress.

Many years ago Captain Jacques Cousteau predicted the coming of *homo aquaticus* — a new race of protohuman with surgically attached fishlike gills connected directly to the circulatory system. Lamentably, fish-gill surgery is not yet an option (although fish-gill tacos are delicious). Nevertheless, inventors have devised an array of ingenious techniques to bring air into water or to extract air from water. For now, however, wannabe menfish will have to make due with tried-and-true scuba gear.

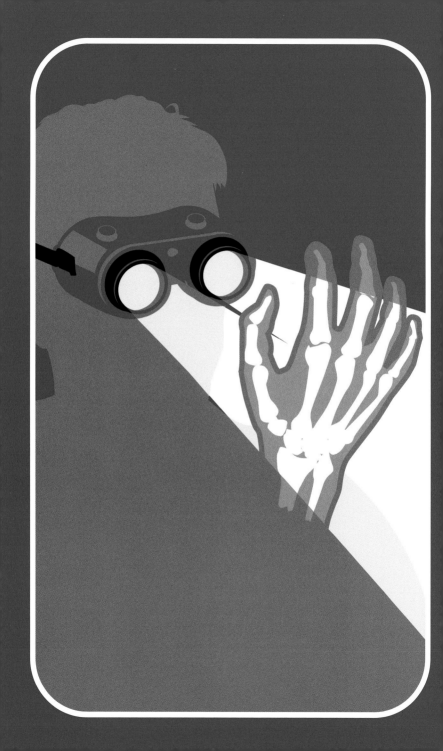

X-RAY SPECS

A lot of promises are made in the bedroom and on the campaign trail, but the biggest, most important promises are made in tiny print on the last few pages of comic books — like the promise of glasses that *let you see through things*. For a modest price these advertisements guarantee the Superman-like ability to see through walls; but honestly, X-ray spectacles were really all about seeing through clothes. The "scientific marvel of the century" offered in comic books may be a gimmick, but modern defense contractors are not playing around.

X-rays are a real phenomenon discovered in 1895 by a German physicist named Wilhelm Röntgen. Wilhelm was experimenting with *cathode rays* (airless glass tubes that discharge electricity) and found that the flowing electron beam caused a certain nearby screen to glow. Like a good primate, Wilhelm promptly stuck his hand in between the beam and the screen and saw the ghostly projected image of his hand bones. After some (more disciplined) experimenting, Wilhelm earned a Nobel Prize and became the father of diagnostic radiology. Later, he helped discover that while X-rays may not penetrate human bone, they are powerful enough to cause radiation sickness, genetic mutations, and possibly sterility — which is why radiologists wear a lead apron over their private bits.

Such safety measures are not necessary on an everyday basis, because light in the visible spectrum is much less powerful than X-rays. That's why we can't see through bikinis — visible light insists on bouncing off even the flimsiest nontransparent objects. Visible light is composed of streams of photons that wiggle in a certain range of frequencies. An X-ray is like visible light except that it wiggles faster — it has more energy. High-energy photons (which are invisible to our eyes) tend to penetrate farther into objects before they bounce off — or they can go all the way through. To develop X-ray spectacles, the trick is to use light with just enough power to penetrate clothing but not enough to penetrate skin. Because let's face it, no matter what the fashion magazines say, walking skeletons are just not that sexy.

The need for better airport security led to the development of a new *backscatter* machine that uses low-power X-rays with just the right finesse — they penetrate clothing but not skin. Specifically, the machine emits and measures the position of X-rays that "scatter back" from a person and generate a photograph-quality image. The process is sometimes referred to by the vaguely disgusting term "backscatting." Very dense objects (like guns) show up dark, medium-dense objects (like skin) come out grayscale, and not-very-dense objects (like clothes) don't show up at all. To summarize, it's a magical machine that spits out naked images of fully clothed people. But a backscatter machine won't fit on your face; it's the size of a refrigerator and takes about eight seconds to scan a person standing about eight inches away.

> **Backscatter machines can see through clothing, but they see through hair as well. Would that good-looking girl you're checking out be just as cute with a shaved head?**

When X-ray eyes leave the realm of gimmicks and enter the local airport, privacy becomes an issue. Who should wield such awesome power? Though backscatter devices are commonly used in prisons, diamond mines, and customs searches, introducing the machines to airports has been a tough sell. Critics warn against bombarding children and adults with X-rays, even low-power X-rays. Meanwhile, the CEO of an X-ray machine company cheerfully reports that radiation levels are similar to that of good, clean sunlight. The American Civil Liberties Union (ACLU) describes the process as a "virtual strip search." Travelers in the United Kingdom, however, are unfazed — virtual strip search machines have been used at London's Heathrow Airport for years.

Despite British nonchalance, in the United States

there exists a new middle ground between security and privacy. "Cloaking" software turns explicit images into something resembling a generic chalk outline of the body while still identifying plastic, ceramic, biological, and other nonmetallic and metallic objects. (Yes, your nipple chains will show up.) The device is not a cure-all, however; a backscatter machine cannot see into body cavities or body folds.

Gawking at naked people is always good fun, but what about using your abilities for the forces of good? Superman used his X-ray vision to see through walls in an endless, obsessive search for truth and justice. Now lowly humans can do the same using the Radar Scope. Research funded by DARPA recently produced the Radar Scope, a device the size of a telephone handset that can sense human beings through up to twelve inches of concrete. The "through-wall personnel detector" uses radar to sense movements as small as breathing up to fifty feet into the next room. Put simply, it is a motion detector that works through walls.

Whether your goal is to see through walls or bikinis, the technology is here. And unlike the swirly sunglasses that disappointed so many of us, these gadgets actually work. Finally, humankind has mastered the power of light and put it to a noble purpose. For around a thousand dollars, you can buy a Radar Scope and dominate future games of hide and seek, but at a reported cost of six figures, backscatter portals are likely to be out of the reach of most comic book readers.

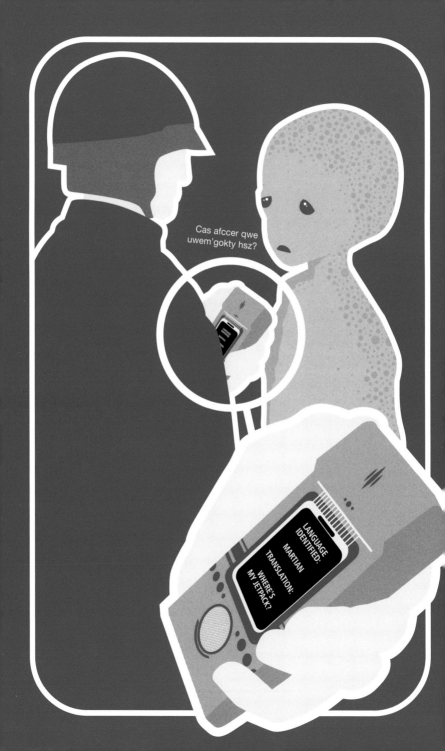

UNIVERSAL TRANSLATOR

The universal translator of *Star Trek* fame made talking to your dog just as easy as talking to Leonard Nimoy. It was small, rectangular, and only vaguely threatening when pointed at a member of an alien race. Though it looked like a foil-wrapped electric razor, it was one high-powered sumbitch — the translator routinely deciphered alien languages and delivered them in the listener's mother tongue. The gadget also picked up *brain waves* to translate languages spoken by creatures with no slobber holes (a paunchy Captain Kirk even used one to communicate with a cloud of gas called the Companion). Luckily, a real-world universal translator has a much simpler problem: it just has to listen to what people say and then translate — no brain waves required.

Over six thousand languages exist in the world, and odds are you only speak one or two of them. A universal translator can help by providing three extremely impressive abilities: speech recognition, language translation, and text-to-speech synthesis. In reality, a universal translator is a wearable computer (a little bigger than a deck of cards) equipped with a microphone (for listening) and a speaker (for spitting out words). Some versions even come with digital cameras that can translate written material or street signs. Many products exist and even more are in the pipeline, so prepare yourself to communicate.

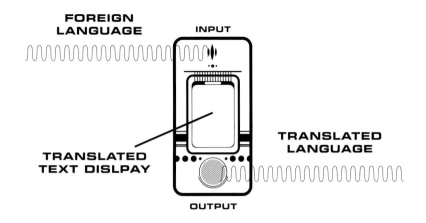

FOREIGN
LANGUAGE   INPUT

TRANSLATED
TEXT DISLPAY

TRANSLATED
LANGUAGE

OUTPUT

The first generation of universal translators are on store shelves, waiting to be purchased by wealthy monoglots. The Phraselator P2 is a pumped-up PDA programmed to translate English phrases into other languages. The Phraselator is deaf and mute, requiring human operators to type in words and then read them off the screen. The Clark County Sheriff's Office in Springfield, Ohio, adopted the Phraselator P2 as a short-term approach to communicating with Spanish-speaking constituents. Police used the device to generate simple phrases like "Hello," "Good-bye," and "Take the bag of kittens out of the trunk, ma'am." Meanwhile, Casio recently produced an electronic dictionary that can say words out loud in six languages: English, Spanish, German, Italian, French, and Chinese. Words must be typed in by hand, but by using text-to-speech capabilities the pocket-sized gadget can speak certain phrases. These devices are impressive (and available), but a true translator will not need a keyboard.

On the battlefield, using your words instead of using your bullets can be exceptionally dangerous. That's why war-zone translators — even electronic ones — are in great demand. The DARPA-funded TransTac system builds on the Phraselator P2 — adding speech recognition and text-to-speech synthesis to automatically translate spoken English into another language, such as Iraqi Arabic, which is then spoken out loud in a computerized (but manly) voice. The system recognizes natural, continuous speech without requiring the user to train it in advance (called *speaker-independent* recognition) and has a lag of about five seconds before translating and saying the phrase out loud in another language. According to soldiers, the machine is more trustworthy than local translators, and it works even when there is background noise or variation in pronunciation. Don't expect deeply philosophical conversations, however; the highly practical device does not translate word for word, but strives to deliver only the gist of what is being said.

Commercially available universal translators are practical and useful, but they fall short of the ideal used in *Star Trek*. The ultimate dream is to be able to translate quickly between every language that exists. Translating all six thousand languages would require almost 36 million translation schemes. However, if every language could be translated to a single universal intermediate language (called an *interlengua*) and then to the desired language, only 12,000 translation schemes would be necessary. By creating a new superlanguage, researchers would remove the need to translate between every single language and reduce the problem to two steps: translating the given language to the interlengua, and then translating from the interlengua to the target language. Many prototypes, including systems from Carnegie Mellon University (JANUS), Fujitsu (ATLAS II), and NEC (PIVOT) use this two-step method. Future universal translators that follow this efficient approach will be able to translate every known human language and will fit in the palm of your hand.

The portable universal translator is extremely useful technology — it could help soldiers and police officers, as well as tourists, airport employees, border patrol and customs agents, and phone operators. As computing power increases and chip size decreases, we may see a future in which a jelly-bean-sized piece of plastic can translate between every known human language. Until then, the most advanced universal translators are battle-hardened PDAs. Instead of reading alien brain waves, real-life universal translators understand two or three languages and allow only very simple conversations to take place. "Donde esta el baño, anyway?"

THE HOME
OF THE FUTURE

ROBOT SERVANT

Human-sized robot servants like Rosie the Robot (of *Jetsons* fame) are clearly the answer to all of life's messes. A household robot is a human-looking appliance that cooks and cleans, offers a helping hand, and handles security. It can understand natural language and pick up and use any tool that a person could. Such a general-purpose robot is more than the sum of its parts — integrating physical dexterity, artificial intelligence, and social skills into one package is a huge challenge. With a potential multibillion-dollar market, however, it is no surprise that robot servants have been promised every decade since 1950. Now, just when you were losing hope that a robot would ever give you a bath, the technology is finally starting to appear.

First-generation robotic servants are available off the shelf. Just follow these three simple steps: Find your credit card, imbibe a half-pint of whiskey, and log on to your favorite shopping Web site. In two to four weeks your filthy studio apartment will be transformed into a futuristic paradise. Robotic vacuum cleaners and tile polishers — available from a half dozen companies — will scurry about, randomly sucking and polishing. Meanwhile, robotic lawn mowers will give your yard an awkward buzz cut (not unlike a blind man with a self-administered haircut). Consumer robots are ready and waiting to change your life for the better.

Robotic vacuum cleaners range in price from a few hundred dollars to a few thousand. These robots are designed for one task, vacuuming; and as a result they all look like low-riding Frisbees. The robots, including the Roomba from iRobot and the Trilobite from Electrolux, scoot around the floor (randomly, for the most part) and vacuum everywhere they go. When they bump into something or hit a drop-off, they change direction and keep going. Like a screen saver that bounces around a computer screen, the robot eventually covers all of an area. Robotic vacuum cleaners not only work well, but also their owners love them — 80 percent of Roomba owners name their vacuums and many repair requests to iRobot are accompanied by a demand to return the original beloved robot, not a replacement unit.

Those sneaky robots are everywhere, even in your own backyard. Grass-munching robotic lawn mowers are more expensive than robo-vacs, but they come with pretty swirling blades. Look for the RoboMow from Friendly Robotics or the Automower from Husqvarna to keep your lawn short and free of pesky neighbor kids. The nearly silent robotic mowers are powered by rechargeable batteries and can handle up to a half acre of grass. A buried perimeter wire keeps the robots from going AWOL. Like vacuuming robots, robo-mowers bounce more or less randomly around the yard, relying on ultrasonic proximity sensors and bumper sensors to detect obstacles. By mowing frequently the overall level of the grass is kept low.

A hardworking auto-mowing machine can only make life worth living for so long. Eventually we need the whole enchilada — a humanoid robot servant. As always, there are teams of bespectacled scientists who are up to the challenge. Humanoid robot prototypes range from doll-size to larger-than-life. A few advanced prototypes can walk, run, and even tromp up and down stairs. Unfortunately, ultra-advanced humanoid robots are extremely expensive and thus often kept on safety leashes, like dogs or small children. In addition, housework is rarely the primary target; most prototypes are designed to look after the elderly or to be walking advertisements for big companies.

Nevertheless, humanoid robot servants are readily available for purchase — in Japan. Mitsubishi sells Wakamaru, a garish yellow robot with a permanent goofy grin. The diminutive robot stands three feet tall and weighs 65 pounds, but it is fully autonomous and can recognize up to ten faces and speak with a 10,000 word vocabulary. The robot has limited mobility because it uses wheels instead of legs, but it has two arms that can grasp objects (like a frosty cold beer). Businessmen at Mitsubishi designed Wakamaru hoping that elderly people would fall all over themselves to live independently at home with the robot instead of going to a nursing home. Wakamaru is cute and safety-conscious, plus it can remind people to take medicine or to attend medical appointments. Meanwhile, another Japanese research team has developed the five-foot-tall, 220-pound RI-MAN humanoid robot, which can pick up and carry a mannequin weighing 77 pounds. The friendly, wheeled 'bot is covered by 0.2 inches of soft silicone skin and should eventually be strong enough to carry an aged relative to bed. Robots and the elderly: two great tastes, together at last!

Other humanoid robots are still in prototype form and too snooty to do much housework. The Honda ASIMO is arguably the world's most advanced humanoid robot, although it is remotely operated by a person hiding behind a curtain. The four-foot-tall humanoid looks like an astronaut and is capable of walking, running (around 3.5 mph), and climbing stairs. The little guy can hold your hand and stroll around, push a wheeled cart, or hand-deliver drinks on a tray. The robot uses head-mounted cameras and microphones to recognize faces, speech, and gestures. A bit of a weakling, the robot can lift only about 2 pounds and lasts forty minutes on a single battery charge.

The Japanese ASIMO has a new friend, HUBO, built at the Korean Advanced Institute of Science and Technology (KAIST). HUBO also looks like an astronaut and stands about two inches shorter than ASIMO. HUBO cannot run as fast as ASIMO, but unlike its Japanese friend, HUBO has eight individually articulated fingers and opposable thumbs, just like a human. This allows HUBO to point and to make very humanlike gestures (yes, even that one). HUBO was recently outfitted with a perfectly realistic android head resembling Albert Einstein. The humanlike head was developed by Hanson Robotics Inc. in Dallas, Texas, using a patented skin material called Frubber. The resulting creature looks as though Albert is back from the dead and dressed like a miniature astronaut. HUBO's body can run for about an hour before it drains its batteries, but HUBO's talking head can last up to two and a half hours. Neither ASIMO nor HUBO are capable of performing chores quite yet, but their physical abilities are approaching human levels.

We don't exactly have a shortage of humans on Earth, and people still have the market cornered on unskilled labor. Nevertheless, you should pat yourself on the back — you were smart enough to be born at a time when human beings are poised to be waited on hand and foot by submissive (and probably not dangerous) robot slaves. Off-the-shelf roboslaves will clean your floors, mow your lawn, and fascinate (or terrify) your children. Meanwhile, advanced prototypes are learning to protect the elderly from a rough, hip-cracking world. In a scant few years, superfuturistic humanoid robot servants are sure to challenge common-law wife statutes across the world.

UNISEX JUMPSUIT

First put on your underwear, then your pants —
modern life can be so difficult. In the future of the
past, however, life was as simple as sliding into a
snug, velvety unitard. The styles of the past were
inspired by something infinitely cool: humankind's
grand exploration of outer space. So cast your fake-
leather fanny pack into the sea, my friend; in the
space-age future you will have no need for pockets,
much less that bulging man-purse.

The advent of space travel introduced a new set of
clothing icons. In the early 1960s the original seven
Mercury astronauts were sporting futuristic, silver
spacesuits. Meanwhile, the Russian cosmonaut Alexei
Leonov was the first human to don a spacesuit and
step outside the capsule for a space walk. These
space explorers bravely faced a new and
unbelievably harsh environment. During an
extravehicular activity (EVA), astronauts entrusted
their lives to a spacesuit designed to allow freedom of
motion and protection from deadly temperatures, killer
gamma rays, and lack of atmosphere. A synthesis of
cutting-edge technology and aesthetics accompanied
the first generation of astronauts into the void and at
the same time inspired a new generation of fashion
designers.

Men and women are equally vulnerable in the
chilly void of space. Possibly as a result, a theme of

androgynous, uniformlike designs soon emerged in circles of high fashion, commercial fashion, and on the bridge of the USS *Enterprise*. Pierre Cardin introduced the Cardin's Cosmos line of clothing, which employed a basic unisex design that could be adapted to accommodate every member of the family. The quasi-military garb was practical, with a focus on mobility — tights for women and trousers for men, topped off with a short tunic worn over a tight sweater. Epaulets were the final touch on this space cadet uniform. Meanwhile, Emilio Pucci clothed the staff of Braniff Airlines in a line of sexy (yet gender-neutral) standardized apparel. Pucci's futuristic designs compelled astronaut Colonel David Scott to offer him a contract to design the official emblem for the *Apollo 15* space mission. Pucci accepted and his design was approved by NASA; Pucci's clothes were literally out of this world.

> **Above 62,000 feet, human beings must wear spacesuits that supply oxygen for breathing and maintain pressure to keep body fluids in the liquid state.**

Most clothing worn by astronauts in space, however, was designed by NASA and aesthetics were not the main concern. Spacesuits require versatile fabrics that can simultaneously insulate the body from the dangers of space and maximize mobility.

Designers caught on to these trends and liberating new clothing lines were cut with an eye toward movement. The prime example of this is the miniskirt — arguably invented by André Courrèges. The miniskirt offers the utmost in freedom of movement (possibly too much for some people). Courrèges's clothes were commonly silver, white, and azure blue to represent the moon, light, and the cosmos, respectively. Famously, Courrèges translated protective space helmets into a line of hats that covered the face, leaving only a slit to peer out of. The translation of space-program necessity into aesthetic apparel culminated in Courréges fashion shows, in which models marched jerkily on and off the stage dressed like a gang of sexy-assed humanoid fembots.

The mid-nineteenth-century era of space exploration and moon landings is the closest that humans have ever come to a true space age, as well as to space-age clothing. Those aging designs from the 1960s represent the ultimate in futuristic clothing and should constitute the majority of any future-naut's wardrobe. It is inspiring to know that at one time the world's most famous designers were consumed with technology and the idea of life in a space-faring future. Designers used aesthetic symbols and technological advancements to envision a beautiful future populated by slim, graceful humans wearing silvery, sexless jumpsuits. Do you think it will ever happen? Fat chance.

SMART HOUSE

Since the beginning of time, children have performed all the duties of a so-called smart home: grabbing beers from fridges, changing television channels, and taking verbal abuse for problems they don't understand and probably didn't cause. Considering that children have been around forever, it is only reasonable to expect that a better technology exists by now. Certainly, we should all be living in robotic houses that act as conscious, living servants to meet our every need and desire.

The now-ancient 1950s image of the "home of the future" was skewed toward rapid manufacturing. The home of the future was designed for mass production, easy transportation, and quick construction; inside, the structure was invariably made of sterile white plastic with built-in furniture and a tiny kitchen. Living in the home of the future was like living in a Swiss army knife. Little did the 1950s denizens know that the true houses of the future would look the same as always, only with something extra that the other houses never had — *brains*.

So, what is the secret to teaching an old house new tricks? One approach is to adopt a do-it-yourself mindset and add futuristic skills like speech recognition (instead of a new patio). There is an entire *home automation* industry ready to supply gadgets that can be integrated to form a soulless automatic home. On the other hand, artificial intelligence can breathe life into a robotic home, allowing it to get to know its inhabitants enough to predict their activities and proclivities. Sinking smart robotics technology into the infrastructure of a home (or spaceship) is called *ubiquitous computing*. Whether you choose home automation or ubiquitous computing or both, don't stop until your house can do a backflip for a mackerel.

Right now, "smart home" technology is available off the shelf; home automation enthusiasts have access to all kinds of gadgets that can make life simpler (and more complicated). The key goal for home automation is to give the occupant total control over the house from anywhere. Most home automation devices require a central personal computer to provide control and to run programs. For instance, X10 modules plug into the wall and then communicate with a home computer, letting a person turn on and off lights and appliances via a Web site. There are quite a few *sensors*, such as cameras, motion detectors, or water leak detectors, that can be used to monitor who is in your driveway, trigger exterior lights when people approach, or constantly check for broken water pipes. Meanwhile, *effectors* can be used to automatically water plants, remotely raise and lower blinds, or feed your pets. Anyone can create the ultimate remote-control house — the only limit is your wallet.

While there is nothing novel about a remote-controlled house, *intelligent environments* are another matter. A whole field of research is focused on blending high-tech computing into the home environment. Instead of interacting with a box on a table, occupants of the future will interact with a helpful, intelligent, and friendly robotic home.

Sadly, fetching your beer is not a priority for smart homes. Instead, the most promising application is to help elderly people live safely and independently. According to census data, within two decades the age demographic of the United States will be the same as the age demographic in Florida today. Smart homes are being designed to use simple sensors common to home security systems and advanced artificial intelligence in order to figure out what people are doing (*activity recognition*) and where they are at (*location estimation*). The Georgia Tech Aware Home looks like a two-story house but is in reality a laboratory bristling with sensing equipment, including cameras in the ceiling, microphones in the walls, and invisible trip sensors in the doorways. The Aware Home and other laboratories like it are the very first prototype smart homes that will help us all stay out of the nursing home someday.

The first series of smart homes is already on the market to help senior citizens live safely in their own homes. The home security corporation ADT recently launched the QuietCare twenty-four-hour monitoring service. This system uses an ordinary home security infrastructure composed of motion detectors and contact switches, except instead of keeping burglars out, the system keeps a close eye on what happens *inside* the house. The system transmits information to

ADT about occupants' daily living activities twenty-four hours a day, seven days a week. Over time, a baseline of normal activity is set and an alarm triggers if the "normal routine" is broken. QuietCare exists so that caregivers and family can lovingly perform a virtual "check-in" with their elderly relative over the Internet. Sounds comforting, doesn't it?

If you are frightened by disembodied voices that emanate from speakers in the walls, then you may want to complement your smart home with a mobile robot. In an experiment with Nursebot (a trashcan-sized, wheeled robot designed to deliver medicine and reminders) at Carnegie Mellon University, researchers found that by using a laser-range finder, a robotic home could correctly predict the paths that people commonly take, so that mobile robots could learn to stay out of the way. Nursebot can use such knowledge to effectively cater to occupants. She even has grab bars so that elderly users can grab hold and stand up. Beat that, Rascal Scooter!

Smart houses are a reality, but most cutting-edge research is designed to make them into babysitters for the elderly. Home automation devices are available, but they require a lot of hard work and the end result is a remote-control house — not a futuristic robotic companion. We can dream of a day when we can ask an obedient house to turn off the bedroom light and instead it makes a pot of steaming noodles, calls the fire department, and then activates a self-destruct mechanism.

WHERE'S
MY JETPACK?

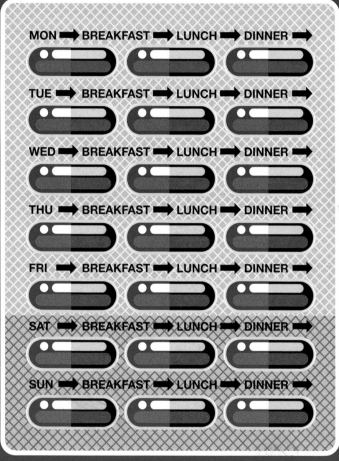

FOOD PILL

Yesteryear's dinner of tomorrow was designed to feed the space-faring denizens of an overpopulated planet. It was cheap, it was synthetic, and it was so completely off the mark as to be almost wholly inconceivable to us now. These days people expect real food from the ground, preferably without any genetic splicing. Overpopulation never happened — populations in the industrialized world are actually declining — but the food predictions of yesterday are as tantalizing as ever. What's more American than an apple-pie pill?

As a rule, future food does not come from the ground. In the best-case scenario it comes from lush hydroponic gardens, but it's much more likely to come from a factory, a tube, or a vat. In addition, future fodder never *looks* like food, either; it looks like a piece of plastic, a splash of corn-syrupy liquid, or — best of all — a tempting little white pill. Put on your bib, because future food is out there and we're going to find it and eat it.

First, let's get this over with — the undeniable, mundane fact is that microwave meals are everywhere. Nuking dinner was made possible by the relatively recent introduction of the microwave oven. A by-product of military research into radar, the first commercial microwave oven was introduced in 1947. It was a half-ton beast the size of a refrigerator and it sold very poorly. By 1975, however, microwaves were small, cheap, and scientifically proven to not cause sterility, blindness, or insanity. Sales skyrocketed and prepackaged *TV dinners* (which had existed since the mid-1950s) became microwavable and began appearing in the freezers of lonely, depressed people worldwide. For better or worse, the common microwave oven heralded the first (and most successful) wave of future food.

Self-heating cans have been around since the early 1900s. Just pull the tab and chemicals mix in a separate chamber, causing an *exothermic reaction* that cooks the can and provides hot coffee, tea, or soup.

The space program kick-started a food revolution. Kids were fascinated with how food got into the astronauts (and how it got back out). Space travelers have serious dietary restrictions: Food has to be as light as possible because every ounce counts on liftoff, and gooey foods are preferred, as renegade crumbs can damage delicate machinery. As a result, early astronauts had to suck food out of tubes and toss back vitamin pills. In the early 1960s, astronauts on the Mercury space missions sucked applesauce out of aluminum tubes. Later, the menu was expanded to include "food powder," freeze-dried food that had to be squirted with cold water and then sucked through a straw. (You can score some of your own from the gift shop at the Smithsonian Air and Space Museum.) By

1965, Gemini astronauts were subjected to Tang, which has the limited advantage of making water taste less like water. Luckily, by 1973, astronauts on the Skylab space station had a luxurious meal-preparation area and a menu with over seventy-two items.

But Skylab did not stop NASA from concocting culinary embarrassments. In recent experiments, NASA scientists have cultured small amounts of edible meat in a lab. The goal is to create *in vitro* meat for human consumption, called *cultured meat*. The advantage of lab-grown meat is that nutrients can be controlled. The use of cultured meat also avoids the common problems of raising and slaughtering a whole lot of hoofed mammals — namely, it reduces pollution from animal waste and eliminates the need for antibiotics to keep animals healthy. The advantages of cultured meat are piling up like white on rice, yet nobody seems to want to actually eat meta-meat.

The problem is a matter of taste. A lab-made meat must have an acceptable flavor sensation — the right smell, taste, and texture. Although a single muscle cell from a cow or chicken can be isolated and divided into thousands of new muscle cells, those cells won't have the right texture without being exercised. So how does a vat-grown meat monster find time to work out? For large-scale production, cells are grown in large flat sheets on thin membranes.

Each thin sheet of meat is stretched (i.e., exercised) before being removed from its membrane and stacked into thick, juicy layers. Alternately, researchers have grown muscle cells on three-dimensional beads that will stretch with small changes in temperature. The full-grown cells are ultimately harvested and turned into a processed meat, like nuggets or hamburger patties. Nothing is as delicious as a freshly killed sheet o'meat. Bon appétit!

Perk up, vegetarians — vegan-friendly organic sludge is literally a staple of science fiction. Raising an animal just to slaughter it is criminally inefficient. Instead, past scientists envisioned streams of algae squirting into molds shaped like cartoon versions of drumsticks and steaks. Algae has a lot of advantages: It is 60 percent protein and is too simple an animal to be easily anthropomorphized. It is also furry, green, and slick. Clearly, delicious microorganisms are the food of the future; yeast, plankton, and algae are all commonly used as nutritional supplements and sometimes even as dinner. The Chinese "vegetable" fat choy is actually delicious *cyanobacterium*. Likewise, the English love their single-celled fungi on toast — Marmite yeast spread is a national delicacy. And let's not forget the Australians and their beloved Vegemite.

But seriously, where are the food pills? The idea is theoretically possible, but like most "technological food," it's not commercially viable. Thankfully, the Combat Feeding Directorate (called *Natick,* after its location) is working ceaselessly to keep U.S. soldiers well fed — and the soldiers have little say in the matter. A decade ago Natick introduced MREs ("meals ready to eat") — individually packaged, self-heating food pouches. Its most recent innovation is the *compressed meal* (CM). A CM is one third the size and weight of an MRE but has the same number of calories. At this rate, the food pill may be on the menu soon. Under the far-reaching metabolic-dominance program, DARPA is soliciting proposals for a pill that will allow soldiers to operate at peak performance during prolonged periods of starvation. Meanwhile, Natick is working on a transdermal nutrient patch that will enable soldiers to go without food for up to three days.

Although military grunts must eat what they are given, the general public seems to hate the idea of nonnatural food sources. For some reason, a bloody hunk of cow meat is more appetizing to most people than a shivering plate teeming with microbial life. Go figure. Nevertheless, many technological foods (including food pills) are either available or under development. For now, you can find the closest food pill equivalent at your local 7-Eleven — go out and buy a HOOAH! brand energy bar; the bars were developed by the Pentagon and have been shown to delay time to exhaustion by about twenty percent.

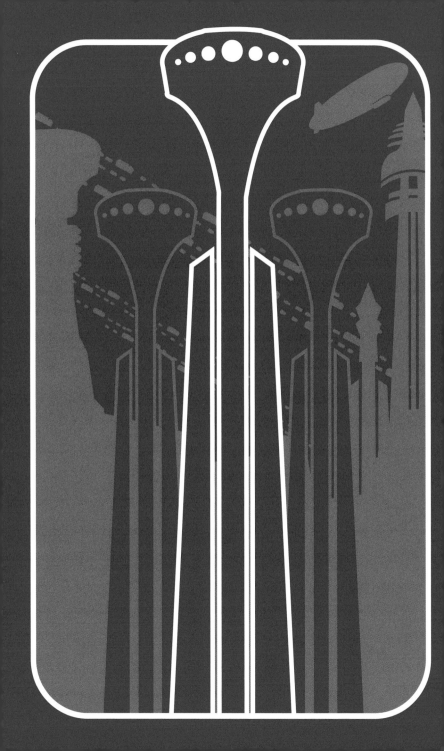

SELF-CONTAINED
SKYSCRAPER CITY

Past visions of the future were technological Utopias — or dystopias, depending on your viewpoint. The self-contained skyscraper city was supposed to house a future population of extremely efficient, highly productive, and very possibly suicidally depressed human beings. When there isn't a blade of grass left, when your "window" is actually a video display piping in a view from miles away, and when there isn't a level below yours because of the molten magma, you'll know that the antiseptic dream of the skyscraper city has been realized.

The film *Metropolis* (1926) depicted a dizzying view of the future city filled with titanic buildings connected by narrow sky bridges and a horizon buzzing with hundreds of autogyros. A similar city was depicted in a 1939 issue of *Amazing Stories*: enormous buildings connected by suspended roadways and riddled with giant aerodromes to house bobbing zeppelins. In these visions of the future, each building was a city in itself, completely self-sustaining, and receiving its supplies from underground trade routes. Agoraphobic inhabitants did not have to go outside for weeks at a time. Smoke was eliminated, noise was silenced, and the sweet air was mechanically purified. The self-contained skyscraper city was a mute tomb of good, clean fun and hard, hard work.

When it comes to modern skyscrapers, people tend to think big. The architect Sir Norman Foster proposed the soaring and conical Millennium Tower for a site in Tokyo Bay and had hoped to build it by the year 2000. It was designed to accommodate 52,000 residents. Measuring 2,625 feet high with 170 stories, the tower would have been three times the height of the Eiffel Tower — if it had been built. Likewise, Le Corbusier fantasized about a "Radiant City" that symmetrically sprouted row upon row of glass-and-steel skyscrapers. Not to be outdone, Frank Lloyd Wright proposed to build a 528-story building, appropriately called Mile-High Illinois, in 1956. All of these proposed buildings included a fully functional ecosystem for inhabitants; they were to contain restaurants, movie theaters, apartments, hotels, and offices— stacked vertically instead of smeared along city blocks. So where are they?

Fully contained skyscraper cities are not quite a reality, but awe-inspiringly tall buildings *have* been built since the turn of the nineteenth century. Known early on as a "high-flying bird" or "a tall hat," the skyscraper was seen as a bold, daring demonstration of American ingenuity. In early America, the steeples of churches were the tallest structures around — closest to the heavens. By the 1850s the state capitols were even higher. But by the 1900s even these venerable structures stood in the shadow of the commercial skyscraper. In an effort to go higher, developers constantly pushed conventional construction to its limit and introduced new methods and materials. In the 1890s, 15 stories was devastatingly tall. In 1913, the Woolworth Building in New York City reached an astonishing 60 stories. This was capped in 1931, by the 102-story Empire State Building, which reigned as the tallest skyscraper in the world for over forty years.

Once an American phenomenon, skyscrapers are now an

international symbol of prestige. For a building to qualify as a skyscraper, the majority of its space must be devoted to human habitation. The height of the building is defined as the distance from sidewalk level of the main entrance to the structural top of the building (not counting antennas or flagpoles). In 2005, the world's tallest skyscraper was the Taipei 101 in Taipei, Taiwan. Built in 2004, the Chinese-architecture-inspired Taipei 101 is (predictably) 101 stories and rises 1,671 feet. The next tallest buildings are the twin Petronas Towers (1,483 feet) in Kuala Lumpur, Malaysia; the Sears Tower (1,454 feet) in Chicago; and the Jin Mao Building (1,380 feet) in Shanghai, China.

The tallest freestanding structure on Earth is the Sears Tower, at 1,777 feet (a third of a mile). The tower has 110 stories that rise 1,454 feet and a television antenna that soars up an additional 253 feet.

Once an astonishing icon of a technological future, the skyscraper has now become a mundane reality. (We are only missing the associated trappings of skyways, speeding air traffic, and gracefully floating zeppelins.) However, life in a fully enclosed skyscraper city is attainable today, although it is not quite as luxurious as predicted. Anyone who wants to become the first citizen of the new skyscraper Utopia should immediately move into an existing skyscraper; dark, cramped apartments are readily available and you can always order in for the rest of your life.

HUMANS ...
IN SPACE!

RAY GUN

The death ray is the logical equivalent of a six-shooter for a hard-drinkin', hard-fightin' space cowboy. In early science fiction pulps, any adventurer worth his space boots carried an old-fashioned holster containing a high-fashion ray gun — and the more stylish the fins, the better. The hardware is now available for us to emulate our cosmic heroes. Pay attention, and the next time you swagger into a tough bar on a scummy planet, the aliens will step back, eyeing your freshly painted, spark-emitting ray gun.

Ray-gun-like weapons are quickly becoming commonplace. Preliminary weapons are nonlethal and have been used by happy-go-lucky military troops and police officers eager to teach new dance moves to protesters and rioters. Several classes of *directed energy* weapons, called *nonkinetic* weapons by military types, have met field trials and are coming into widespread use.

The Active Denial System, developed by the Pentagon, can aim and emit super-high-frequency microwaves (even more powerful than your favorite hotdog cooker). When the millimeter-sized wave pulses hit human skin, they heat the body's water to the point of pain. The burning sensation has been compared to touching a hundred-watt lightbulb, but without the singed hair — the system is only playing with your nerve endings, not causing permanent damage. Currently, the weapon won't fit in your holster— soldiers have to mount them on top of Humvees.

If you want to make the upgrade from Active Denial to Active Cookery, you'll need to petition DARPA to let you

FFZZT

borrow the Vigilant Eagle, a weaponized high-power microwave (HPM) device. The defensive weapon looks like a pair of highway billboards leaning against each other (nearly indiscernible from common radar) and is designed to confuse incoming shoulder-fired antiaircraft missiles. Once a target is identified (for example, a chicken potpie), the fully automated HPM device steers a short-duration pulse beam that engulfs the entire target, cooking any delicate electronics (or tasty cubes of processed chicken). The HPM focuses energy to within a one-degree angle, which can send a damaging electrical pulse into computers and guidance systems. If the HPM radiates in the wrong direction, however, the beam flies away harmlessly — the energy quickly dissipates to about the power of a cell phone call. When the HPM is properly targeted, its range is several miles and the system requires less energy and less accuracy than a laser weapon.

Alternately, why not use a prototype "lightning gun" to harness the Zeus-like power of electricity? A host of new defense contractors have sprouted to help governments battle terrorists, and they supply a variety of hair-raising weapons. Companies like Ionatron and Xtreme Alternative

URF!

Defense Systems (XADS) have developed competing zap guns. Both weapons use pulsed lasers to create a conductive path in the air away from the gun's barrel and then use a simple Tesla coil to generate a painful bolt of electricity. Both rifles are the size of a briefcase, weigh twenty-five pounds, and can shoot electricity wildly at twelve feet or consistently at four feet. Occasionally, the flashing purple discharge kicks back and lashes the bejesus out of the poor guy holding the gun.

We have so far ignored the most compelling directed energy weapon of all — the laser blaster. Jedi Knights can apparently use lightsabers to easily deflect laser bolts, but electrically driven solid-state laser weapons (preferred over their less-wieldy chemical-based cousins) are designed primarily to zap approaching missiles. Field-tested military prototypes are pushing 25 kilowatts of power and research is underway on versions that can turn missiles into Swiss cheese with 100 kilowatts of laser power (a million times more powerful than an everyday laser pointer). For reference, surgical lasers generally use about one tenth of a kilowatt of power to cut through human skin.

Meanwhile, the General Atomics company has

developed a prototype weapon, called the High Energy Liquid Laser Area Defense System (HELLADS). Precise details are classified, but the system purportedly combines two types of laser, liquid and solid-state, for a single überpowerful weapon. Unlike liquid lasers, the HELLADS can fire a continuous beam without a large cooling system, and unlike solid-state lasers, the HELLADS produce a high-energy density that does not require pulsing the laser on and off. The whole system weighs 1,600 pounds and can fit into the space of a large refrigerator. The project goal is to eventually spit a 150-kilowatt beam clean through enemy missiles.

> **Testing futuristic laser systems in the United States must be carefully timed so that stray energy beams — designed to burn through rocket motors from miles away — do not accidentally chew through expensive orbiting satellites.**

The big question, of course, is what is keeping a handheld laser blaster out of your pocket? The most noticeable obstacle is heat dissipation. Operational lasers are inefficient, converting only about 15 percent of electrical power into laser, with the rest wasted in the form of extreme heat. More efficient *diodes* (the part that converts electricity to light) would lower heat output and shrink lasers so that they could hang jauntily on your hip. For now, though, you will have to be happy with mounting military lasers to your tactical ground vehicle (that's your Buick).

SPACE MIRROR

Around a hundred million miles from Earth a ferocious, sustained nuclear reaction is happening. The sun has been pouring energy into our planet for billions of years, and since the dawn of science fiction, humankind has yearned to master that power. Hugo Gernsback believed that mirrors hanging in space would create an eternal spring for happy earthlings. Space pioneer Hermann Oberth described a devastating weapon that might incinerate entire cities. In fact, the first orbiting "death star" became fully operational over two decades ago.

A German physicist, Hermann Oberth was a founding father of rocketry and astronautics, but he made more than rockets. In the 1920s, Oberth devised a dead-serious scheme for placing a giant mirror into Earth's orbit. The proposed mirror was to be up to 100 miles in diameter and composed of lightweight, paper-thin squares of highly reflective metal. Each silvery square could be aimed so that the solar energy reflected by the mirror could be diffused over wide regions of Earth's surface or concentrated into a single flaming pinpoint. Oberth imagined great and terrible uses for the space mirror, but he may not have imagined that it would be deployed well before the end of the century.

An international race for a space mirror was in full swing by the late 1960s. In 1967, NASA and the Department of Defense proposed Project Able. The project intended to put an inflatable space mirror into synchronous orbit. On command, the satellite would expand into a 2,000-foot disk and begin using attitude control jets to illuminate a circular area of Earth approximately 220 miles in diameter with twice the brightness of a full moon. Ostensibly, the technology would provide a peaceful means to illuminate sun-starved cities during the winter months, light up disaster areas for search and rescue, and provide *solar sails*, which might reflect sunlight to propel spacecraft into deep space. In reality, the Vietnam War was on and critics saw only military applications. Not surprisingly, the project set off a worldwide storm of controversy.

Soon after, Russia declared its intention to pursue a space mirror as well. The world recoiled upon hearing that two superpower nations had plans to employ godlike space mirrors. The Cambodian government immediately lodged a protest to the United Nations Security Council. Meanwhile, the international scientific community mounted an intensive campaign to regulate the deployment of bright objects in orbit. Scientists feared that night light would unbalance natural circadian rhythms, disrupt the weather, and infest the sky with "light pollution." A proposal to the United Nations to protect the night sky was introduced. It seemed that Oberth would never realize his simple dream of an armored space station with the power to destroy planet Alderaan.

Faced with heavy opposition, NASA and the

Defense Department dropped the plans for a space mirror. However, the crafty Russians did not cave in to worldwide pressure from pesky political and scientific communities. In the early-morning hours of February 4, 1993, a patch of reflected sunlight emblazoned the night sky and shone on Earth. This seemingly divine miracle was caused by Znamya-2 (the *Banner*), a Russian solar sail positioned in orbit 225 miles above the ground. The slowly spinning satellite unfurled a razor-thin reflecting film that stretched 66 feet in diameter but projected a weak 2.5-mile-wide beam of light at a leisurely 5 mph across a sleeping Europe. The pulse of light lasted only six minutes and was about as bright as the moon (1 lunette). More controversy followed, but the next Russian space mirror was already under development.

Six years later, the new prototype was ready to deploy. The Znamya-2.5 solar sail was intended to be 83 feet in diameter and to beam a circle of light about 3 miles wide, moving at 14 mph. The aluminized plastic sheet was only 7 microns thick but its beam was to be five to ten times brighter than Znamya-2's. As the delicate satellite began its slow-motion emergence from the Mir space station, a communications antenna mistakenly began to extend. The nine-pound plastic and aluminum mirror became entangled, and collapsed uselessly against its mothercraft. Astronomers rejoiced and the setback sent the Russian space mirror program into obsolescence.

The outlook for space mirrors is bleak, but an alternative is within reach. The *heliostat* is a mirrored device placed high up in order to reflect the sun's rays to more useful places. For example, in New York City there are three heliostats (each about 8 feet in diameter) atop a twenty-three-story building that provide sunlight to the skyscraper-enshadowed Teardrop Park. The computer-guided mirrors automatically track the movement of the sun and send down a meager circle of light onto a park bench or tree. Meanwhile, in Rattenberg, Austria, an entire city is enshadowed by mother nature's skyscraper — a mountain. The town has mounted thirty computer-controlled mirrors (each about 8 feet square) a half mile north. These mirrors reflect sunlight to another collection of mirrors on a nearby hillside. On cloud-free days the computer-controlled heliostats beam in sunshine to a dozen selected "hot spots." Heliostats are a pale imitation of orbital reflectors, but they get the job done for now.

The sun is such an integral part of life that using science to redirect sunlight has intrigued (and terrified) people for generations. Controversy has stifled innovation in space mirror research before; however, humankind is slowly, inevitably spreading into space. Someday, our artifacts will be common inhabitants of the now-virgin night sky. Whether space mirrors are used for peace or war, let's just hope that the horizon stays free of advertisements for "enlargement" pills.

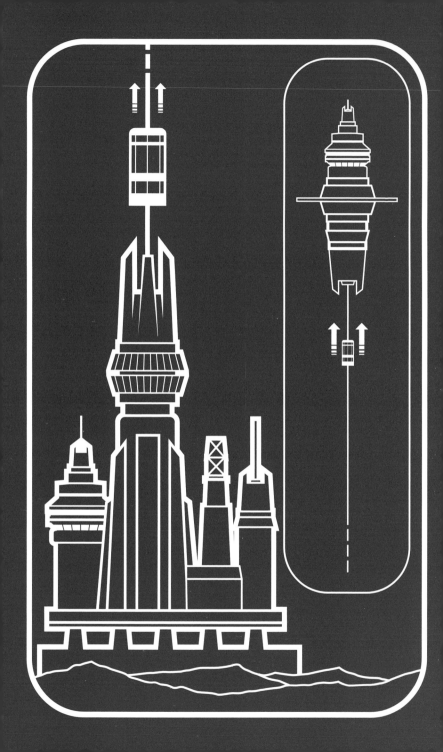

SPACE ELEVATOR

The first public elevator was installed in the year 1850. Within fifty years, inquisitive scientists took elevators to the next logical level — outer space. Scientists examined the feasibility of an elevator stretching into orbit, and what they found may surprise you: Theoretically, there is absolutely no reason why a *space elevator* should not work. What began as an entertaining mental exercise has now become a legitimate scientific goal. Physicists, roboticists, and material scientists are collaborating on a mind-blowing project to build a vertical mega highway to space.

As early as 1895, Russian scientists were discussing a fanciful "Celestial Castle," a huge tower in geosynchronous orbit attached to Earth by a strong cord. By the 1970s, sci-fi authors such as Arthur C. Clarke were weaving stories around superelevators that could smoothly lift a payload of people or parts into orbit. Science and science fiction often collide, and soon after their appearance in sci-fi stories, space elevators began to be mentioned in technology journal articles and at scientific conferences. Physicists concluded that no physical or economic reasons existed for not seeing a space elevator in our lifetime. A path to the stars began to unfold.

The space elevator is composed of four main parts: a tethered end on Earth, a cable, a tethered end in space, and a powerful robotic lifter to carry payloads from one end to the other. The proposed cable is really a three-foot-wide ribbon, thinner than a sheet of paper and about 62,000 miles long. Crane your human neck, because that is a fair distance; the average orbiting height of the U.S. space shuttle is about 200 miles. One end of the cable is attached to Earth's bellybutton (the equator) and the other end is anchored in space by a huge weight (around 600 tons). The counterweight will chill out in space at nearly a fourth of the distance to the moon, which orbits Earth at 237,674 miles. A robotic lifter climbs the cable, hauling tons of payload for a fraction of the price it would take to launch on a rocket. The lifter is expected to cruise at around 100 mph, requiring only a few hours to leave the extreme upper atmosphere (about 300 miles up at the equator). The whole majestic machine would be in perpetual balance with the rotation of the planet.

For perfect balance, the space elevator would be tethered to our planet near the equator; an equatorial location is aligned with geostationary orbits and has the best weather. However, it is not mandatory that the cable stay in any particular spot. Plans call for the cable to be rooted to a mobile anchor ship in the ocean. The huge, floating platform could move at any time to relocate the elevator in order to dodge space debris or dangerous tropical storms.

A superstrong cable is the most important and challenging piece of the plan. A study conducted by the U.S. Air Force shows that the maximum stress on a space elevator cable is in the middle, at geosynchronous altitude (around 22,000 miles). Because it will be stretched from both ends, the cable material must be thicker in the middle and taper exponentially toward the ends. A sufficiently strong material with an adequate taper ratio has never existed — until now.

> **Using today's energy costs, researchers estimate that the cost to transport a pound of material into orbit by shuttle is around $10,000. On the other hand, a space elevator is estimated to lower that cost to around $100 a pound — or less.**

Carbon nanotubes were discovered in 1991 by Japanese researcher Sumio Iijima. Carbon nanotube composite ribbon is the perfect substance for a space elevator; it is lightweight, one hundred times stronger than steel, and as flexible as plastic. Nanotubes are composed of a highly ordered sheet of carbon atoms that have been rolled into a tube shape. The whole tube is as small as one nanometer in diameter and only a few nanometers long (one thousand times narrower than a human hair and invisible to the naked eye). The microscopic nanotube fibers are set down side by side and woven together to form a growing ribbon (researchers at Los Alamos National Laboratory have grown them longer than four centimeters). The only drawback is cost — at current prices the material for a long enough nanotube cable would cost over a billion dollars.

If we could afford one, a space elevator would be truly awe-inspiring. Standing Earth-side, the ribbonlike cable would stretch straight up through the clouds. As the planet rotates, inertia at the end of the tether would counteract gravity and keep the tether stretched taut (with about 20 tons of force pulling upward). The robotic lifter would take a scant few minutes to ascend through clouds and climb higher than Mount Everest, until the curvature of Earth would become visible. Low-Earth orbit (a few hundred miles up) would be riddled with lethal debris and satellites. Luckily, the North American Aerospace Defense Command (NORAD) already tracks orbiting objects larger than 10 centimeters (3.9 inches). At around 22,000 miles up, the robotic lifter would be safe, rotating in lockstep with satellites and debris that share a geostationary orbit. Even so,

don't expect to hang out on the observation deck —
the space elevator would run through a region of high
radiation called the Van Allen belt.

But what about when the whole affair inevitably
goes wrong and Jack's beanstalk is cut? If the space
elevator were cut in the middle at a high altitude — up
to around 15,500 miles — the lower portion of the
cable would fall while the counterweight would
jettison into space. Don't worry about falling debris,
the ribbon would be so thin that it would burn up
spectacularly in the atmosphere. If the tether were cut
here on Earth, the outward force exerted by the
counterweight would yank the whole chili dog into
outer space. The same principle could be used
intentionally — climbing to the end of the
counterweight and letting go would catapult an object
into deep space.

Space elevators are theoretically possible and yet
they do not exist. To be perfectly honest, it's your
fault. Anyone can join in on space elevator research.
NASA and the Spaceward Foundation have teamed
up to offer $400,000 in prizes to teams that develop
winning space elevator designs. Anyone can submit
designs that solve two different pieces of the space
elevator puzzle: increasing tether strength and
improving power transmission. Join a team and make
it happen — if you won't do it for science, do it for the
cold hard cash.

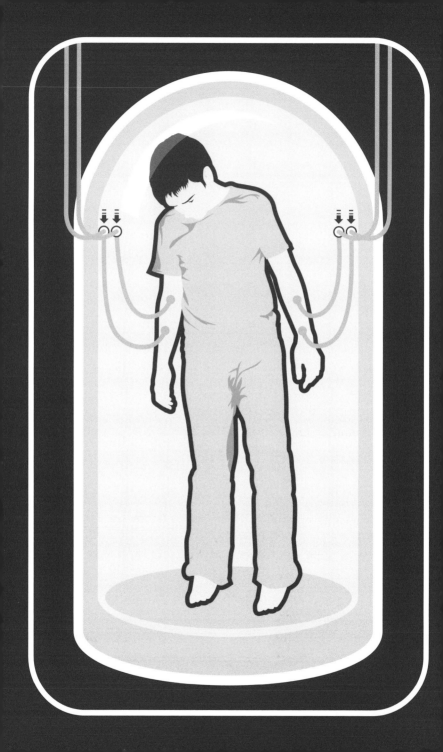

CRYOGENIC FREEZING

Futuristic space travelers are commonly frozen for eons-long journeys in science fiction novels. So why is your head not frozen right now? Because you are still alive? Poor excuse. You have the potential to take a quick trip into the future and here you are palming a silly book with your meaty human paws. You *could* be a thousand years in the future, standing in a thin atmosphere and cradling a mutant human baby with your horrific titanium claws. Or not. Regardless, the need to be frozen for the future is inescapable, so here are the details:

The idea behind cryogenic freezing is simple: In order to live long enough to see a cure for genital herpes, we must freeze ourselves and preserve our bodies for some future scientist to unthaw and revive. Afterward, it's all free love and running through rainbow-filled meadows. That is, unless you can only afford to have your head frozen and not your entire body. Then it's all about lipping a straw and sipping Courvoisier by a swimming pool. The question is not *whether* to become a frozen dinner, but *how*?

Cryogenics is a branch of physics concerned with generating and studying very low temperatures. *Cryobiology* is an area of cryogenics that studies the effects of low temperatures on biological organisms, usually with the intent of cryopreservation. Despite the occasional caveman lawyer that pops out of a frozen glacier, this is a complicated scientific field. The first cryonic procedure occurred in 1967 and since then over a hundred people (everyone knows that heads count as people) have been put on ice, with a thousand or so more signed up but not dead yet. Cryobiologists routinely freeze and recover free-floating cells and tiny clumps such as embryos, but freezing and reviving whole organs (or organisms) is outside the reach of current technology. Cryonics (the science of freezing and thawing whole organisms) is a *proto-science*, based on expectations of the repair capabilities of future science. Keep in mind that the previous sentence is in the small print of every cryonics commercial.

Somehow, we have reached an age in which, when it comes to freezing your body or just your head, we have plenty of options. There are dozens of companies that will turn you into a human corpsicle and store your chilled earthly remains indefinitely. The process is as follows: First, your still-warm corpse is gradually chilled in an ice bath; after being treated with an anticoagulant your blood is replaced with a preserving solution to minimize damage from freezing; your corpse is further cooled to minus 79 degrees centigrade with dry ice; and over a period of five days further reduced to a nippy minus 196 degrees in liquid-nitrogen-filled flasks. At this temperature a slight knock will literally shatter your dreams of living forever. All corpsicles are stored head-down to minimize the risk of damage to the frozen brain in the event of a power loss and subsequent melting. You are now a human Popsicle and you are going to stay one until scientists perfect the fine art of reverse human Popsicle-ization.

Freezing is the easy part. Rejoining the human race may be much harder. The freezing process is extremely

damaging to human tissue, shriveling cells and squashing them between sheets of ice and pools of chemicals used to minimize freezing damage. A frozen brain generally has ripped axons, hemorrhaged capillaries, unraveled myelin, extruded cell contents in the extracellular space, and other gross alterations. For this reason, most experts doubt that human memory can survive cryosuspension. Specialists believe that cryonic suspension — while not necessarily a scam — is almost surely a total waste of money, space, and energy. Nevertheless, let the worms go hungry; the chance of being reborn in the future as a brain-dead humanoid zombie surely beats having no chance at all.

Although many of us certainly would like to be frozen immediately, alas, it is illegal. A corporation may not legally cryopreserve a living person and it is especially illegal to perform neurosuspension (freezing just the head) on a living person. Instead, we will have to wait giddily for death and our chance to live in the future. Plus, once you are on ice, your family will be welcome to come out and stare at your condensation-covered freeze tank. (Unfortunately, they will not be able to gaze at your horrifically mutilated, chilled corpse — unless they can see through your polished steel coffin.)

MOON COLONY

In 1969, Neil Armstrong danced a jig on the lunar surface and unleashed moon mania on the world. The *New York Times* predicted that happy colonists would be bounding hand in hand across the moon in twenty or thirty years. The centerpiece of Disney's Tomorrowland attraction was the luxurious Moonliner spaceship. But a future that included giant glass moon domes never appeared. Tomorrowland was torn down. Now, almost a half-century later, our attention has returned to the sky — humankind is finally going back to the moon.

The Apollo missions put twelve people on the moon between 1969 and 1972. Around that time a moon colony was not only possible; it seemed inevitable. The General Electric company proposed building a moon colony using two hundred Saturn V rockets (under development for the Apollo space program). The prescient GE plan was to boost equipment to the moon robotically and then to follow up with more precious cargo — ten human colonists. The colonists were to construct a base from the equipment before building return vehicles for the journey home. Translucent domes and cheery gardens were mandatory.

Obviously, moon colonies currently exist only on the drawing board, but the time is nigh for a homecoming. In 2005, NASA announced a master plan for returning humans to the moon by 2018. The plan is simple, straightforward, and not much different from the original Apollo program. It does not involve teleportation or space catapults. In fact, the plan does not even call for additional funding — just a drastic realignment of priorities. Every last NASA scientist, contractor, and international collaborator is now singly focused on that pale orb; by the end of the next decade the moon will be home to four determined humans.

Populating Luna with moon men will require two new space vehicles: one big ol' rocket to carry people and equipment into orbit, and another spaceship to journey to the moon and back. Say good-bye to the current generation of winged, reusable space shuttles — they are cruising toward the junk pile. A new generation of semi-reusable *crew exploration vehicles* (CEVs) are about to be phased in. The CEV is modular, with pieces built for housing astronauts during the journey to the moon (the *exploration vehicle*), ferrying astronauts from moon orbit to the lunar surface (the *lunar lander*), and a propulsion system for cruising between Earth and the moon (the *Earth departure stage*).

NASA hopes to kick off the moon mission by putting a massive 358-foot, 6.4-million-pound cargo-launch vehicle into space. Lifters must first carry every piece of the crew exploration vehicle (including the crew) into orbit. The huge rocket will be powered by towering solid rocket boosters, and astronauts will rest snugly in the nose cone during liftoff. The experience will be safer than flying in airplanelike space shuttles: Future astronauts will be packing parachutes and can bail at the first sign of trouble. After launch, most of this majestic missile will be jettisoned into space or burned

HERE MEN FROM PLANET EARTH FIRST SET
FOOT UPON THE MOON JULY 1969 A.D.

WE CAME IN PEACE FOR ALL MANKIND

up in Earth's atmosphere, although the CEV can be recovered and reused up to ten times. Once in space, the exploration vehicle will romantically mate with the lunar lander and the journey to the moon can begin.

The final game plan may sound familiar: The moon rocket will ignite and carry the exploration vehicle (and four astronauts) on a three-day trip to lunar orbit. Afterward, the craft will (intentionally) split into two pieces: The exploration vehicle will orbit the moon while the crew of astronauts boards the lunar lander and travels to and from the surface. The new lunar lander is better than the one used by Apollo astronauts; it is larger, carries twice as many people, and can support them on the moon for months instead of days. Other improvements include a lighter, stronger structure, more-efficient propellant, and the ability to land anywhere on the moon, instead of just on the equatorial plane. Do not worry about that unmanned exploration vehicle orbiting overhead; it will be piloted by trusty robots. Let's just hope that NASA doesn't use the dreadful Heuristically programmed ALgorithmic computer (HAL) 9000 — that guy has a terrible safety record.

Robots are doing more than piloting spacecraft — they are astronauts too. NASA is testing Robonaut, a humanoid robot that will work hand in hand with flesh-and-blood astronauts. From the waist up, the 225-pound Robonaut is a dead ringer for a fully suited astronaut, capable of using screwdrivers, squeezing through hatchways, and clasping the ubiquitous handgrips essential for locomotion in zero gravity. If commanded, the robot can visually locate and pick up a power drill before threading and screwing on a bolt. The Robonaut is one tough hombre — it can work in the void of space where an unprotected human would simply explode.

The new lunar party pad will be a home base where astronauts can study the moon, test new equipment, and mount the trophy heads of sliver-toothed "Moon Wyrms," which they have defeated in low-gravity combat. Astronauts can also plan a more ambitious journey to Mars. The moon may be our first stop, but Mars is the final destination. NASA believes that moon-livin' astronauts will be well prepared to live off the land during future missions to Mars, using machinery to collect solar energy and raw materials for construction. With the moon as a stepping stone, we may finally reach the red planet and bring our precious Mars rovers back home — they haven't been fed in years.

CONCLUSION

In the distant, hazy past — when humanoid robots were hand-carved out of wood and laptop computers were powered by steam — people dared to dream of a future in which technology conquered all. Hopefully, in this book you have caught a glimpse of the Utopia promised by our science fiction forefathers. You can rest well knowing that you can man a zeppelin, build your own hoverboard, or pilot a jetpack. Whether these technologies are present or not, they must not be lost to time.

We are up to our necks in half-baked technology of the past: Space vacations are possible if you are a multimillionaire; deadly ray guns are available but they are the size of cannons; and just a single underwater hotel serves as a vacation destination for the entire world. Even teleportation is a reality, but only one photon at a time. These partially realized mechanical miracles do not represent defeat; they reflect the bone-grinding determination of scientifically minded men and women everywhere. Scientists are tenaciously delivering science fiction promises — all so that you can suck on an algae-sicle before being cryogenically frozen and going on a space vacation in a solar-mirror-powered spacecraft.

But incredible past advances in technology are not enough. We cannot sit by idly while our children walk

to school instead of riding hoverboards, while newlyweds spend their honeymoons in aboveground hotels instead of in underwater hotels where they belong, or while our grandparents are forced to eat full meals instead of choking down handfuls of food pills dispensed from a slot in an otherwise featureless wall of solid granite. The course of action is clear: We must educate ourselves, stand up for ourselves, and fight for the future we were promised.

It is not enough to wonder "Where is my jetpack?" Instead, you must grab your favorite scientist by the lapels and shake hard. Never stop pushing the frontiers of science, never lose your natural human curiosity, and never give up. Get out there, raise your voice, and demand your personal jetpack — the magnificent future of humankind depends on it.

ACKNOWLEDGMENTS

Thanks to Anna Camille Long for reading this book more than once. The woman can now pilot a zeppelin, hoverboard, or jetpack like nobody's business.

To my family in Oklahoma, especially my grandparents Genieve Wilson and Jim Meadors (who are not afraid to spread the word to local newspapers), my parents Dennis and Pam Wilson, my little brother David and his wife, Mindy Wilson, and my pal Tanner "The Tan-Handler" Rogers.

To my wonderful agents, Laurie Fox and Justin Manask.

To my aggressive editors, Panio Gianopoulos and Colin Dickerman.

To my "no holds barred" publicist, Yelena Gitlin.

To Richard Horne for illustrating this little slice of the future.

Special thanks to my friends and colleagues who contributed their expertise: Brenna Argall, Chris Atkeson, Mark Baumann, Colby Boles, Paul Brown (author of *The Rocketbelt Caper*), Larry Carroll's Girlfriend, Peter Diamandis, Yes Duffy, Brad Edwards, Abraham Flaxman, Peter Gijsberts (www.rocketbelt.nl), Juan Pablo Gonzales, Matt Hancher, David Hanson, Melissa Herman, Stuart Heys, Brian Russell Long, Michael Loop, Brett Lundmark, Amalia Marino, Rande Shern, Dan Stern, Alik Widge, Mike Winters, and Jie Yang.

And thanks to all the scientists, inventors, and tinkerers out there. **Please hurry up.**

A NOTE ON THE AUTHOR

Daniel H. Wilson earned a Ph.D. in robotics from the Robotics Institute of Carnegie Mellon University. He is the author of *How to Survive a Robot Uprising*, winner of the *Wired* Magazine Rave Award for best book of 2006. He laughed out loud at every joke in this book (even the terrible ones).

Daniel lives in Portland, Oregon.

www.whereismyjetpack.com
www.danielhwilson.com

A NOTE ON THE ILLUSTRATOR

Richard Horne is a designer and illustrator whose work includes record and book covers, Web sites, greetings cards, and newspaper and magazine illustrations. He illustrated Daniel Wilson's *How to Survive a Robot Uprising* and is the author of *101 Things to Do Before You Die* and two more books in the *101 Things* series.

Richard lives and works in East London.

www.101thingstodo.co.uk
www.homepage.mac.com/richard.horne